SHAKESPEARE: THE MERCHANT OF VENICE

by
A. D. MOODY
Lecturer in English, University of York

EDWARD ARNOLD

ISBN 07131 50920 Boards
ISBN 07131 50939 Paper

Printed in Great Britain by
The Camelot Press Ltd., London and Southampton

General Preface

It has become increasingly clear in recent years that what both the advanced sixth former and the university student need most by way of help in their literary studies are close critical analyses and evaluations of individual works. Generalisations about periods of authors, general chat about the Augustan Age or the Romantic Movement, have their uses; but often they provide merely the illusion of knowledge and understanding of literature. All too often students come up to the university under the impression that what is required of them in their English literature courses is the referring of particular works to the appropriate generalisations about the writer or his period. Without taking up the anti-historical position of some of the American 'New Critics', we can nevertheless recognise the need for critical studies that concentrate on the work of literary art rather than on its historical background or cultural environment.

The present series is therefore designed to provide studies of individual plays, novels and groups of poems and essays, which are known to be widely studied in sixth forms and in universities. The emphasis is on clarification and evaluation; biographical and historical facts, while they may of course be referred to as helpful to an understanding of particular elements in a writer's work, will be subordinated to critical discussion. What kind of work is this? What exactly goes on here? How good is this work and why? These are the questions which each writer will try to answer.

DAVID DAICHES

Contents

Contents

1. Introduction

The present standing of *The Merchant of Venice* is about as puzzling as its meaning. It is one of the best known of Shakespeare's plays; and, as it seems to me, it is possibly the least well understood. Its familiarity is the result of its popularity as a school text; its being generally not fully understood may stem from the same cause. Certainly the expectations brought to it, and the level at which it is commonly read, even among advanced commentators and critics, seem to be those established in and for the schoolroom. A related fact, whether consequence or cause or both it would be impossible to tell, is that many of the more serious and respected Shakespeare critics have paid little more than passing attention to the play. (In particular one would like to have had something sustained from L. C. Knights and Derek Traversi, whose particular approaches are the ones most obviously missing from the discussion.) It would be a fair generalisation that the play has not received the full and serious attention that it deserves. I would like to think that in time it will be seen to be at least as closely related to *Henry IV* and *Much Ado about Nothing*, the plays it probably just preceded, as to the earlier and slighter comedies with which it is more often associated.

The established view of *The Merchant of Venice* goes something like this:

> *The Merchant of Venice*, then, is 'about' judgement, redemption and mercy; the supersession in human history of the grim four thousand years of unalleviated justice by the era of love and mercy. It begins with usury and corrupt love; it ends with harmony and perfect love.[1]

Professor Frank Kermode, whose formulation this is, supports it with the assertion that 'only by a determined effort to avoid the obvious' can one fail to see that that is the meaning of the play. I have to confess that what seems to me obvious, is that the promised supersession of justice by love and mercy does not come about, and that the end is something of a parody of heavenly harmony and love. The play *is* about the qualities he

[1] *Early Shakespeare* (Stratford upon Avon Studies: 3, Arnold, 1961), p. 224.

mentions, but it treats them much more critically than he suggests. He
seems to have overlooked the irony that is at the centre of its meaning.

To emphasise the importance and centrality of the irony, I would
suggest that the play is 'about' the manner in which the Christians
succeed in the world by not practising their ideals of love and mercy;
that it is about their exploitation of an assumed unworldliness to gain the
worldly advantage over Shylock; and that, finally, it is about the
essential likeness of Shylock and his judges, whose triumph is even more
a matter of mercenary justice than his would have been. In this view the
play does not celebrate the Christian virtues so much as expose their
absence.

Yet this account too, though no less true than the more usual one,
would be less than adequate to the experience. For the special quality of
the play is that it refuses to endorse any such simple judgements. It com-
pels an intensely sympathetic insight into Shylock's tragically corrupt
nature, yet we are unlikely to identify ourselves with him. It reveals in
the Christians a complacent inhumanity, and yet we are likely to find
them attractive in their fashion. No account of the play which offers to
see it in terms of simple good and evil can hope to satisfy. It is too subtle
and exploratory for that; and also, perhaps, too ironic in its resolution.

A 'prima facie' Reading

The characterising quality of the Venice–Belmont set is their worldliness. This makes it odd that their claims to represent the Christian virtues
should be accepted at face value. With the exception of a few set pieces
on the themes of mercy, love and harmony—and of Antonio's partial
representation of these qualities—their minds are never raised above the
gaieties and good things of the world.

Their way of life and the things which possess their imaginations are
suggested in the opening exchange:

Solanio.   Believe me, sir, had I such venture forth,
           The better part of my affections would
           Be with my hopes abroad. I should be still
           Plucking the grass to know where sits the wind,
           Piring in maps for ports and piers and roads:
           And every object that might make me fear
           Misfortune to my ventures, out of doubt,
           Would make me sad.

Salerio.   My wind, cooling my broth,
            Would blow me to an ague when I thought
            What harm a wind too great might do at sea.
            I should not see the sandy hour-glass run
            But I should think of shallows and of flats,
            And see my wealthy Andrew docked in sand,
            Vailing her high-top lower than her ribs
            To kiss her burial. . . . Should I go to church
            And see the holy edifice of stone,
            And not bethink me straight of dangerous rocks,
            Which touching but my gentle vessel's side,
            Would scatter all her spices on the stream,
            Enrobe the roaring waters with my silks,
            And, in a word, but even now worth this,
            And now worth nothing? (I. i. 15-36)

In image and idiom that splendidly evokes the merchant's compulsive fears and hopes, and his world of profit and risk. The language of the play as a whole is drawn quite consistently from that world, so that the action is firmly placed in a context of worldly preoccupations and values. Venice and Belmont emerge as gay, splendid and rich, and not very near to heaven; their end is profit and pleasure, not perfection.

One set of words recurs constantly in their speech—*venture* and *fortune*, or *hazard*, *chance*, etc. From the recurrence comes a cumulatively powerful sense that the goal of their endeavours is the winning, metaphorically and literally, of the 'golden fleece', a common image for the great fortunes the Elizabethan merchant-adventurers hoped for. But to be committed to the pursuit of worldly fortune is to be subjected, in the medieval view of things, to the whims of the fickle goddess Fortune; at the most serious level, it is to forfeit the redemptive influence of Providence for the chances and reverses of Fortune's wheel. Boethius' salutation to the true followers of Christ in the world, 'O happy race of mortals if your hearts are ruled as is the universe by divine love', can scarcely be applied to the Christians of Venice and Belmont. The fount of their happiness is Portia, appropriately referred to as a golden fleece of fortunate beauty and wealth. In consequence their allusions to the values of a world transcending their own, such as divine mercy or heavenly harmony, stand out as precisely that, allusions to quite another world.

But more than this, their worldliness is shown to be of a kind which subverts their religion. In the passage from Salerio quoted before, what we have is not a simple preoccupation with the world, but the expression of that preoccupation in an idiom adapted from the pulpit. It was commonplace to draw from the hour-glass the moral that man's life is brief and eternity his proper end. But Salerio reverses the preacher's logic and draws a wholly secular moral, ignoring any life beyond death. Again, his culminating image, 'Enrobe the roaring waters with my silks', very strikingly fuses the splendour and the loss, but without at all heeding the implicit biblical admonition against the vanity of rich apparel. The whole passage is, in effect, a parody of orthodox warnings against putting one's hopes upon worldly fortune, since it echoes them only to reduce them to an occasion for a more anxious concern with the world.

The major instance of this irony is the contrast between Portia as we see her at Belmont, lightly disregarding the bonds of law and duty, and as we see her in the court, disguised as the wise doctor of law. One observation will be enough to suggest how grave the disparity could be, and to what ironic effect. When Portia declares near the end of IV. i, 'I was never yet more mercenary', there is a curious and significant effect. The immediate sense, quite innocently playful, is clear enough. And yet 'mercenary' is a startling word to have just there, the more so as it echoes 'mercy', which would have seemed the obviously appropriate word. Behind the echo, as it happens, lies the fact that both words come from the same Latin root, *merces* (reward or fee). The direct, secular, development was to 'mercenary', meaning 'actuated by self-interest'. But at the same time, through the influence in Christian Latin of the complex of ideas implicit in the Redemption, 'mercy' came to mean 'pity or compassion' of the sort shown, in its supreme form, in Christ's so loving the world as to die that it might be redeemed from sin. All this is manifestly very relevant to our thinking about Portia, in which a main question must be whether her conduct conforms to the ideal of loving one's neighbour as oneself, or is more nearly self-interested. Coming where it does, with its oddness and ambiguity, that 'mercenary' crystallises the suspicion that what we have seen in her is perhaps literally mercenary, and that her appearance as Justice and Mercy has been a most deceiving disguise. There is then a possibility that Portia has outdone even the Venetians in subverting religion to her own worldly will, reducing its supreme principle of generous love to something nearly its opposite. *Can* Portia be said to love Shylock as herself, or as she loves her Christian friends?

However, this ironic questioning of Portia, though it is pervasive, is unlikely to lead us to reject her. What it should do is prevent the uncritical acceptance of her at face-value. After all, one of the main themes of the play is that 'the world is still deceived with ornament', and the action is constantly exploring the ways in which the appearance and the reality may differ. The warning to be not beguiled by 'the seeming truth which cunning times put on/To entrap the wisest' is surely as relevant to Portia, in her borrowed robes and with her 'gracious voice', as it is to Gratiano in his assumed 'civility' (II. ii. 174ff.). Shylock's image of 'Christian fools with varnished faces' may be apt in more ways than its context at first suggests.

A word here about the way the allusions to the Christian ideal work in the play may prevent some misapprehensions. It is not easy to gauge the exact force of these allusions, partly because they are so variable a quantity, shifting from a subdued presence in Salerio's opening speech to the explicitness of Portia's invocation to Mercy. But it is possible to be definite on the main point, and that is that the Christian ideal is not deployed as a standard by which the characters are to be judged. The controlling viewpoint is not that of the eye of Heaven, but that of enlightened human feeling.

There is a neat illustration in Lancelot Gobbo's choosing Bassanio's world, at the expense of his duty to Shylock, in terms which evoke a morality-play frame of reference (see II. ii. 1-29). In fact we don't judge him as a Christian soul, but simply as a sly rogue with an eye for the main chance. The judgement implied by the allusion to the morality play, that he is damned if he do not repent, is distanced and dissolved in the clowning. All that remains of it is a clearer definition of his motives and conduct as a young man in the world of men. It is the same with the Christians in general. The play does not imply, for example, that they ought to be ideally merciful; nor that they are damned for falling short of the ideal or subverting it. The dramatic experience simply does not lead us to judge them in relation to the ideal; it leads us to judge them by their treatment of Shylock. Their offence is not against God but against humanity. The function of the allusions to the Christian ideal is to sharpen our awareness of the human issue, but not to be a measure of it. Their function may be likened to that of the coloured spectacles that went with the early 3D pictures: when one looks through them the images assume definition and depth. They are there to be looked through, not to be looked at. (There will be more to say in the concluding chapter on the manner in which the play works by and for an enlightened sense of human values.)

The need for a detached and critical approach is brought home still more when we consider Shylock's part. For while he is grievously wronged by the Christians, to the extent that his inhumanity is effectively their doing, he must nevertheless be held fully responsible for the inhuman act he proposes. Yet again, while the judgement the Christians pass on him is fully deserved, we cannot but feel that his humanity is larger in scope and depth than theirs. In consequence his defeat at their hands seems to involve a reversal of the right order of things, the lesser being allowed to put down the greater.

John Russell Brown has shown that in the theatre it has always been Shylock's play,[1] and there is good reason for this. Where the Christians speak with quibbling wit or rhetoric, filtering emotion through artifice, Shylock's speech is directly responsive to his burden of personal and racial experience, with the result that his humanity is so much more fully present to us. To take just one instance. In III. i he answers Salerio's 'thou wilt not take his flesh—what's that good for?' with this terrible directness: 'To bait fish withal! if it will feed nothing else, it will feed my revenge'. This reveals far more than the mere desire for revenge. There is an element of wild desperation, indicating the root of that desire in some deep outrage or frustration; and there is a despairing sense of the futility of the revenge, since the pound of flesh cannot heal the real hurt. Through the intense realism of his image we can feel the fermenting pressures which have made him what he is. He is no simple devil or machiavel, but a man who sees and feels and thinks as other men do, except that his feeling and thinking has been terribly twisted by the wrong done to him. As Traversi wrote, Shylock 'is one of the first of Shakespeare's characters to require of us, like so many of the later tragic heroes, a response in which different and even contradictory judgements are simultaneously evoked.'[2]

All this must complicate and deepen the interest of the play beyond

[1] 'The Realisation of Shylock: a theatrical criticism', in *Early Shakespeare* (Stratford upon Avon Studies: 3).
[2] *The Pelican Guide to English Literature: 2*, p. 185 (q.v.).

any simple issue of the good *v.* the damned. The play confronts us rather with the triumph of a group of worldly and a-moral characters over one whose evil is inseparable from his larger humanity. There is much that is baffling in this spectacle of the breaking by a set of trifling gilded youth of a man with something of the stature and interest of a tragic figure. But we must not attempt to evade or to oversimplify the experience. It is only by making sense of what baffles us that we can attain a full understanding of the play.

Romantic Idealism in the Received Readings

'The good group stands for the code of the gentleman and the gentlewoman: loyalty, charity, courtesy, hatred of evil . . . Shylock is a thoroughly evil monster.'[1] 'Shakespeare would have written a satire on Christianity had he intended it to be represented by those characters who are hostile to Shylock' (Heine).

First impressions should be enough to suggest that the first quotation is a gross simplification, and that the second is rather nearer the mark. Yet most critics would agree with the first rather than the second.[2] Most have looked for such simple readings as it suggests, and judged the play a success if they found one and a failure if not. Those who respond to Shylock's disturbing stature only conclude that 'poetry and plot are at odds' (D. J. Enright),[3] and that it 'does ill-service to the play as a whole' (J. R. Brown). Those who recognise the levity and worldliness of the Christians remain confident that that could not have been Shakespeare's meaning. Either he has failed, they argue, or we need to find some rationalisation which may explain how the imperfections of the Christians are really their virtue. Most critics, in short, seem to want the play to show, or at least to have been meant to show, good triumphing over evil in something like the ideal vision suggested by Professor Kermode.

Behind most of these readings there appears to be some romanticising or idealising impulse, a wish to find in the play an assurance that the world may be simple and good, in spite of its evidence to the contrary.

This is very clearly the case in 'Q's' introduction to the Cambridge New Shakespeare edition. He charges Shakespeare with missing half

[1] Leo Kirschbaum, *RES*, XXI, 1945, pp. 136-42.

[2] The critics mentioned in this section are taken to represent the large majority of those who have written on the play. For details of the writings directly referred to see 'Note on Texts and Criticism'.

[3] *The Pelican Guide to English Literature: 2*, p. 416.

the point when he makes the Venetians 'as a class and by habit, just as heartless as Shylock'. Shakespeare should have made them ideally charitable, it seems, in perfect contrast to Shylock's cruelty, and in perfect accord with the idyllic romance 'Q' finds in the last act. But is not this self-declared romanticising?

> One would like to believe that against Venice with its moral empti-
> ness, Shakespeare consciously and deliberately opposed Belmont
> (the Hill Beautiful) as the residence of that better part of the Renais-
> sance, its 'humanities', its adoration of beauty, its wistful dream of a
> golden age. . . . The Fifth Act redeems us into a world in which good
> folk are happy with free hearts that move to music. . . . We have been
> won back to a saner, happier acceptance of life. (pp. xxx-i)

More recently romantic or idealist readings have become more scholarly and more sophisticated. One of the most influential has been E. C. Pettet's discussion of the play in the light of the conflict in Eliza-bethan society between the ideals of Christianity and the practices of capitalism. His account of this conflict provides an illuminating historical context, but his finding in the play an 'ideal' resolution of the conflict, with disinterested generosity triumphing over self-interested money-values, seems to me not to correspond to its facts. The value Shylock puts on his pound of flesh is, surely, quite the reverse of monetary. So far as I can see the victors are not less self-interested than their victim— after all, it is they who show a profit on the trial, the bond not met and Shylock's goods to boot—and the function of the ideal they appeal to is to point up this irony.

The same sort of thing has to be said of Professor Nevill Coghill's argument that, if only we make ourselves Elizabethans and orthodox Christians, we may see in the play this triumphant reconciliation of Justice with Mercy:

> We return to Belmont to find Lorenzo and Jessica in each other's
> arms. Christian and Jew, New Law and Old, are visibly united in
> love. And their talk is of music, Shakespeare's recurrent symbol of
> harmony.

One has to accept Lorenzo as a statutory Christian, but there's not much to identify him with any law, let alone the New Law. As for Jessica, has she not been accepted as a 'gentile', and precisely in recognition of her considerable breach of justice? Professor Coghill's reading seems to require us to stand off at some distance from the play, and to abstract from it or to impose upon it an ideal sense which may indeed have been entertained by good Christians and which is certainly alluded to in the play, but which is at odds with the experience it actually offers.

In spite of that we find Professor Kermode saying very nearly the same thing. And J. R. Brown improves upon Pettet as well as Coghill in describing the play as a joyful celebration of 'Shakespeare's ideal of love's wealth'. Then there is C. L. Barber who in effect incorporates 'Q' as well. He finds in the play a high civilisation, based on but transcending wealth, which opposes a faith in 'community and grace' to Shylock's supposed money-values, and which is vindicated in the 'cosmological music' and 'universal harmony' of the last act. He finds it a play 'completely without irony about the joys it celebrates'.

To be able to do that one must have the advantage of a highly selective filter. Mr. Barber's is efficient to the degree that the doubts he admits to, in a vague afterthought, don't get into his picture at all. Mr Brown does notice that in the last act there is 'wrangling and talk of cuckoldry and unfaithfulness' (Arden edition, p. xlix), but without any sense that this might tarnish 'the moonlight and talk of harmony'. Others have observed the heartless levity and predatoriness of the Christians, or that Jessica is a renegade and a thief, or that Portia's speech tends worryingly to the artificial; or, most disturbing of all, that Shylock is grievously wronged by the Christians' justice and mercy. Yet these observations, which are dropped in a random way by the romantic and idealist critics, as well as being made by those who resist their readings, seem never to be gathered together, nor allowed to accumulate their due challenging weight. That in itself indicates the strength of established romantic and idealist *Gestalten*, their power to see through or to explain away what doesn't fit their preconceived image. The conviction that Shakespeare could not have written a satire on the Christians seems able to withstand even the experience of the play itself.

Some notice needs to be taken of the quite respectable and plausible methods by which the play may be made to seem other than in itself it really is. They may be observed in the arguments used to justify the Christians' judgement on Shylock. The difficulty for the idealist reading was well stated by E. M. W. Tillyard:

When Antonio and the Duke in their mercy force Shylock to turn Christian, surely we are meant to recall Portia's pronouncement that

B

you cannot force mercy. . . . In my heart I cannot help thinking that
Shakespeare must have intended some ironical contrast between
Portia's ideals and the cruder understanding of the Venetians.[1]

One might wonder, by the way, what reason there is to suppose
Portia's understanding of the ideals she has pronounced to be less crude
than that of the Venetians—see IV. i. 374-89. One might add as well a
question about the apparent irony in Antonio's having refused Shylock
(in I. iii) the fellowship he is now forcing on him.

The difficulty is usually met by a recommendation that we see the
play with what are supposed to have been Elizabethan eyes rather than
with our own. The Elizabethans, we are told, would have thought the
Jew quite handsomely treated. Witness the anti-semitism exhibited in
the case of Roderigo Lopez, Portuguese of Jewish descent, physician to
the Queen herself, who was publicly hung drawn and quartered in 1594
upon suspicion of plotting against her life. Witness the 'Elizabethan
standards' by which 'Shylock had no hope . . . of entering a Christian
eternity of blessedness [since] he had not been baptised'. From Antonio's
point of view, therefore, as Professor Coghill sees it, 'Shylock had at
least been given the chance of eternal joy'. Unfortunately both these
arguments are unsound even in their own terms; and if they are not
convincing one must suppose, since they are advanced by very intelligent
people, that they have not been reasoned out from the given evidence,
but are rather rationalisations of a prior conviction. In any case they
represent a kind of argument which is of very dubious value for literary
criticism.

Take them first on their own terms. So far as the baptism issue goes,
the fully orthodox belief was surely that no man receives the sacrament
against his will; but that any man who freely and with right intent wills
to be baptised must, in one form or another, receive the sacrament. It
would seem then that Antonio is not giving Shylock any opportunity he
had not had all along, in principle. Moreover the main effect of his
forcing the baptism, must be to make it as difficult for Shylock to want
it as had his previous spurning of him. Antonio *may* not have been acting
in hardness of heart, but nor was he acting in Christian sympathy.[2]

---

[1] *Review of English Literature*, II. iv, 1961, p. 59.
[2] On the matter of 'Elizabethan standards' it should be noted that in
The Jew of Malta (I. ii) enforced conversion is unequivocally a punishment
for recalcitrant Jews. An interesting survey of the relevant historical and

As for the trial and execution of Roderigo Lopez, the apparently scholarly critics can hardly be said to have done more than seek confirmation for a favoured hypothesis. Other and conflicting interpretations are possible and should surely be taken into account. The appointment of a Portuguese Jew as the Queen's physician could suggest that Elizabeth herself was not dominated by the alleged Elizabethan antisemitism; and if so, might not the same have been true of Shakespeare? Then, since what was said at the trial is not to be trusted, might it not have been his nationality as much as his race that exposed him to the suspicion of plotting, at a time when Protestant England's most virulent fear was of Catholic Europe? Again, to take a line directly relevant to my reading of the play, it seems possible that to a well-informed contemporary the main interest in the affair could have been the part played by Essex. According to Dr. Dover Wilson 'the trial and conviction of the Jewish doctor were due to the exertions of Essex, who owed him a grudge and who presided over the judicial proceedings' (New Shakespeare ed., pp. 116-17). If we are to conjecture a connection between the trial and *The Merchant of Venice*, we have as good reason to suppose that Shakespeare was concerned at a possible subversion of justice, as to suppose that he would simply endorse the façade of legality. And, if so, we must suppose him capable of as readily condemning as condoning the unjust and merciless execution of an alien.

There is another hypothesis which, if we are to be impressed by this kind of argument, might as well be advanced in support of my reading. Professor William Empson has recently reminded us, in a related context, that 'the English felt culturally and socially inferior beside the Italians and Spaniards, and felt it a duty to try to catch up; but also took comfort in remembering that we were good and they were wicked, partly because they had such a wicked religion. Webster would be astonished to have his Italians taken for Englishmen.'[1] Might not Shakespeare have expected his Italians likewise to seem splendidly and fascinatingly wicked? We can be fairly certain in any case that the Christians of Venice and Belmont would not have been taken by Shakespeare's Protestant audience for the Anglo-Catholics which, to adapt Professor Empson again, 'the neo-Christian critics have to pretend

literary background may be found in H. Sinsheimer's *Shylock: A History of a Character, or the Myth of the Jew* (London, 1947).
[1] *Essays in Criticism*, XIV. i, 1964, p. 81.

that everybody has always been'. All this puts the enforced conversion of Shylock in another light again. Would the Elizabethans have been so Jesuitical as Professor Coghill? Might they not have thought rather of the Inquisition and their own Bloody Mary? Ought we perhaps connect Portia with the Scarlet Woman of Rome?

It would perhaps be safer to conclude that the only conclusion we can safely draw from the historical evidence is that in itself it is inconclusive. Empson put this rather nicely: 'the idea that everyone held the same opinion at a given date, "the opinion of the time", is disproved as soon as you open a history book and find a lot of them killing each other because they disagreed.'

There is another more general and more important point. Even were it proved that Shakespeare's audience were anti-semitic to a man, and believed naïvely in the efficacy of enforced baptism, it would not follow that Shakespeare was a typical Elizabethan. A great writer is never the simple register of the received opinions and emotions of his time; if he were he would be on a level with the diarists and pamphleteers. The great writer is distinguished by a capacity for giving a new form to the mind of his age. Our expectation should be that Shakespeare's expression of the mind of his age would be not inert but exploratory and creative; and we should expect to find him challenging the common attitudes of his age with his extraordinary insight.

It follows that historical evidence (which would include the 'sources' of the play) is helpful in precisely the way the dictionary is helpful: it may prompt us to perceive new or unfamiliar meanings, but only within the context of the work itself can we know which meanings are the relevant ones. The business of criticism is to seek the truest meaning which the play itself prompts and supports. While it is true that the more knowledge and experience we bring to it the richer our reading is likely to be, the larger truth is that the meaning, the significant structure of thought and feeling, resides in the play and not anywhere else. If we would avoid being misled by our own preoccupations, ideals and dreams, or by even the soundest scholarship, we must submit our minds to the experience of the play, and make our criticism an articulation of that experience.

It may save a certain amount of irritation with the discussion that follows if I frankly declare one at least of its limitations. I am conscious of having consistently emphasised the ironic rendering of Venice-

Belmont, and of having perhaps left the elements of Renaissance and Christian Romance to speak for themselves. I have no fear of their being overlooked, especially since they have been so generally and so persuasively recommended to our notice. So generally and so persuasively that it seems necessary to stress the ironic element very firmly indeed to have it noticed at all, and to have any hope of bringing about a more justly balanced view. A study such as this is not addressed to *tabulae rasae*.

2. *The Play*

1. *'Friends that purpose merriment'* (*I. i-ii*)

Antonio's 'sadness' is like a keynote sounded before the statement of the play's main concerns. Later, as it persists through the scene, it becomes an undertone set off against and showing up the levity of his friends. The word 'sadness' had a primary meaning of 'sober, grave, serious', and would signify that Antonio was preoccupied, withdrawn into himself. The cause is nowhere plainly stated. Instead our interest is shifted to his friends; but in their inability to respond adequately to his mood we begin to see its meaning. He is sad, in the modern sense, because his more sober, grave and serious feelings are unrecognised and unsatisfied. His passive demand for a deeper understanding and friendship meets no response—being beyond matters of fortune and merchandise it is beyond the Venetians' comprehension—so that even among his 'friends' he is an alien. The prime interest of this is in what it suggests about them. It will be relevant to recall it later, when we find Antonio failing to recognise or to respond to Shylock's implicit demand for friendship. But for the moment Antonio's 'sadness' is a foil to his friends' trifling worldliness.

Here, as later in the trial, he is the curiously still and passive centre of the scene. His presence seems to have the odd function of declaring some absence or emptiness, making us aware of some hollowness at the heart of Venice. He is, in his effect, a dumb reminder of unrealised possible feelings, of deeper needs and impulses than any Venice is aware of. In this there is again a parallel with Shylock's fate.

The Venetians seem to circle about Antonio like quick indifferent creatures of another element. Theirs is the world of wit and pleasure-seeking, and it is to the exploration of this world that the play is mainly devoted. The substance of I. i and ii reveals it in its several aspects. There is first the parodic relation of its worldliness to religion, as shown in Salerio and Solanio; this is capped by Gratiano's 'sermon' upon the impropriety of 'sadness'; then Bassanio carries their attitudes into action, and finds their proper object in Portia.

Gratiano is the main spokesman and effective philosopher of the Venetians' worldliness. He will be found to be, throughout the play, a sort of nether touchstone for the Christians, giving expression to their basest elements. His advice here to Antonio, on how to be worldly without letting its risks and dangers prevent merriment, is the complement to Salerio's solicitude, and is in the same idiom. 'You have too much respect upon the world' appears to look for a more religious conclusion than the sophisticated 'They lose it that do buy it with much care', which is a neat conversion of 'What shall it profit a man if he gain the whole world and suffer the loss of his own soul?' Gratiano proceeds from this to make explicit the previously implied preferences for the folly of the world, rather than the wisdom of heaven. His attachment is to the liver, 'the supposed seat of love and violent passion' (SOED), and to the life of the warm blood; and he mocks the filial and traditional pieties represented by 'his grandsire cut in alabaster', the effigy on the tomb.

His most revealing piece of wit is his parody of Antonio's 'sadness'. Here he represents at its crudest the Venetians' shallowness. To assume that Antonio must be pretending to be 'sad' in order to deceive the world is firstly a blind failure of sympathy. Secondly, it shows an inability to conceive the possibility of genuine seriousness; and to this he adds the expectation that an appearance of gravity is something to be exploited for an ulterior motive. He himself has this use for it when he agrees to 'put on a sober habit, . . . Use all the observance of civility,/Like one well studied in a sad ostent/To please his grandam' (II. ii. 174-200).

In all this Gratiano is making explicit the attitudes of the worldly Christians, revealing in a crude and unmistakable form what is more subtly present in the rest. He is the shallow cynic to whom nothing is sacred or even serious. All that is real to him or important is 'merriment', which seems to amount to a vulgar knowingness, cheap witticisms and the bawdy punning he contributes to the love scenes. The darker aspect of his shallowness, is shown in his grotesque preaching at Antonio's 'sadness'; and of his cynicism, in his readiness nevertheless to pretend to sadness for gain. In these latter respects he prefigures, and so 'places' in advance, such things as Antonio's misinterpreting Shylock's need for love as greed for money, and Portia's putting on a sober habit 'With purpose to be dressed in an opinion/Of wisdom, gravity, profound conceit'. Not only the nature of the Christians' attitudes, but even the actions in which they will issue, are being foreshadowed.

Bassanio, despite his attempt to dissociate himself from Gratiano before Antonio, is manifestly cast in the same mould. His constant association with him later in the play is a persistent reminder of this. He shares the same 'enlightened' worldliness, and his end is likewise 'merriment'. But he is like Gratiano in nothing so much as his capacity for cynically using serious emotions which he does not share. In his exploitation of Antonio's generous love he acts out the Venetians' incomprehension of its value, and their parodying or subverting things of profound value.

Nothing so positively demonstrates the nature and depth of Antonio's 'sadness', his serious and unsatisfied need to love and to be loved, as his deliberately offering Bassanio not only his purse but his person. Bassanio takes full advantage of both, in order to venture for Portia and her fortune, and in doing so casually reduces the personal love to a merely monetary value. This is most clearly evident in the way his urgent self-interest quite blinds him, in I. iii, to the implications of his bonding Antonio to Shylock. If Shylock puts his daughter on a level with his ducats, Bassanio likewise puts Antonio's money before his person. This is the worst parody or perversion so far wrought in Venice, (the trial has yet to show what can be done with Mercy), that the profoundly human affection, which transcends their preoccupation with the world of fortune, should be exploited in the pursuit of fortune, and subjected most rigorously to the cold chances of Fortune.

In his relation to Antonio Bassanio appears as something other than the resplendent venturing lover. The shallowness of his feelings, already apparent here, will become shockingly clear in his exaggerated and empty protestations at the trial (see IV. i. 111-13, 279ff.). It would be not inappropriate if his name came to be suggestive of baseness, in the sense of 'opposed to high-minded'; and perhaps also to suggest the bass, 'the common perch', which catches the shallow and callow aspect, and also 'a voracious European marine fish', which catches the more serious underside. The effect of these things upon our sense of Antonio's love is to emphasise about equally its nobility and its pathos. The role his love is to be allowed is already fully prepared· its best expression can be only to die for Bassanio's selfish sake.

It needs little comment that fortune and fortune's wealth, as these are represented by Portia, are the great themes of Bassanio's talk. Some of the implications of these preoccupations were noted earlier. The point to be added here is that in this the revelation of Venetian worldliness is carried beyond its negative or subversive effects to the positive good which is its end and object. Portia is presented as the fulfilment of their affections and desires. She is characterised by wealth, beauty and virtue, in that order. The last is perhaps not above question. Her 'fair speechless messages' are not quite in keeping with the claim that she is 'nothing undervalued/To Cato's daughter, Brutus' Portia'; the paragon of cold roman chastity thus invoked could hardly be so warm and welcoming. Not that there is anything wrong with such warmth in itself; but if so unlikely an account is given of it, it must make it seem such a melting of marble into blood as Gratiano would approve. The surer emphasis thus falls on her wealth and beauty, the attributes which make her 'a golden fleece' whom 'many Jasons come in quest of'. This is unmistakably to introduce Portia as fortune's prize for adventurers.[1]

In appearance she should be dazzlingly eye-catching, a striking justification of Bassanio's account of her. Her hair, which is much emphasised—'her sunny locks/Hang on her temples like a golden fleece' —would be the red-gold known as 'sunny-blond', and would be 'crispéd' in the style shown in such paintings as Bartolomeo Veneto's 'Portrait of a Courtesan'. Her dress too would be elaborate and splendid, in a courtly style, showing her to be the beautiful prize which attracts 'renownéd suitors'. At the same time of course she is young and high-spirited, as her talk shows, visibly chafing against such formality, wanting to let out the hoydenish element apparent in her wit. This contrast between her appearance and her talk is of the first importance

[1] The mythological allusion is more ironic than dignifying. Jason's qualification as an adventurer was his freedom from moral scruple. The more interesting implication is that if Portia is to be carried off by a Jason, then she is not the golden fleece merely but also Medea, who broke her father's law and used magic arts to enable Jason to steal the fleece, on condition he took her too.

in a production, since it gives a visible hint of the division which is the essential thing in her character.

The first words of Portia, who has won the affections Antonio cannot command, recall his but with a difference. She is weary through surfeit, boredom and idleness; her tone suggests a fever of the blood, 'love-sickness' rather than settled and deep affections. In idiom and feeling she quickly associates herself with the sophisticated and cynical Venetians. Her first retort to Nerissa's mild reproof reduces morality to rhetoric; and she goes on to give an account of how morality fares in the world, which is in effect an exercise in worldly wisdom designed to excuse herself from any duty to live above the world. Its main statement directly echoes Gratiano's on the difference between blood and alabaster: 'The brain may devise laws for the blood, but a hot temper leaps o'er a cold decree'. Her mock-virtue is in his vein too—she will *seem* demure and virtuous to the end she may get her a husband. There is every reason to see her as close kin to the Venetians, in putting merriment and pleasing her own will before all else, and in being willing to put on sobriety only to pursue those same ends. Her difference from them—and the tone here is much lighter, more simply comic and pleasant, and without any of the selfish cynicism which tends to sour scene i—can be accounted for by her not being put in relation to any Antonio. There is nothing here seriously to touch or question her levity.

Her wilfulness is measured only against her father's will—'so is the will of a living daughter curbed by the will of a dead father'. The punning here is quite penetrating. In the one case 'will' extends beyond 'last will and testament' towards the sense of a bounden duty to treat such a will as sacred. In the other it takes the opposed sense, beyond 'wilful' towards implications of self-willed pleasure or passion or lust. This is treated very lightly. At the same time we are invited to see, though without attaching much weight of feeling to the perception, that her enforced subjection to the will of her dead father is exactly the predicament mocked by Gratiano, and that it must challenge a hot temper to seek a way to evade it. All that the present scene shows in this respect is that she will take such playful precautions as she may to prevent those she does not favour from choosing the right casket. Her vow that she will 'die as chaste as Diana' unless she be obtained by the manner of her father's will should perhaps be taken equally lightly. It seems rather to express relief at the discourage-ment of unwelcome suitors than any strict sense of duty; moreover her response to Bassanio's name is in another tone, and one which suggests where her 'will' lies. Her sense of duty promises to extend only to keeping the letter of her father's will. (Here we touch the sense in which she may be associated with Medea.)

A curious incidental aspect of Portia's being made the prize in a lottery, and one which underlines her attitude to her situation, is that it places her in a predicament roughly parallel to that in which Antonio is shortly to place himself. Both are to be subjects in law to fortune. But there is this difference, that whereas Antonio freely accepts the bond, Portia cannot help feeling that she may need to outwit her father's will. This has a clear relevance to her intervening to deliver him from his bond: she at least does not feel circumscribed by law.

Portia's witty comment upon the Prince of Morocco at the close of the scene is one of those light remarks, so characteristic of the more purely comic element in the play, which carry a most muted and yet most reverberant significance: 'if he have the condition of a saint, and the complexion of a devil, I had rather he should shrive me than wive me'. It seems to invite no more than sympathetic laughter. Yet the mocking indifference to inward worth, following upon her fondly recalling the unworthy Bassanio, just glances at the quality of her loving what pleases the eye, a thing to be remembered when we come to the song about 'Fancy' in III. ii. There is a more direct relevance which would emerge as soon as Shylock comes on a few words later. If a dark complexion is taken as the sign of the devil then this dark-skinned alien must come under the ban of the same prejudice. In fact, though they are said so lightly, Portia's words do exactly anticipate the quality of the Venetians' attitude to Shylock, and serve to lead us back quite naturally into their more disturbing world—naturally, because hers has been only a lightened version of that world.

2. *Shylock's Instruction in Villainy* (I. iii; II. ii–vi, viii; III. i)

Mr. Graham Midgley[1] has drawn attention to the likeness in one main respect of Antonio and Shylock—both are aliens in Venice. It seems to me that there is a profound dramatic basis for this likeness. Antonio, who is an alien *within* his society, may be seen as an image of the inoperancy

---

[1] Other points in this section have been anticipated by H. C. Goddard and J. B. Shackford. For the relevant publications of all three see 'Note on Texts and Criticism'.

of love in the hollow heart of Venice. Shylock who is put *outside* that society, and who shows the full effects of its defective love, may be seen as the image of what happens within the human person when love is denied, of the consequent distortions and corruptions of feeling and impulse. Thus he and Antonio face each other as the social surface and the inward substance of the same spiritual condition. If that is too metaphysical a way of putting it one can say, more simply, that with the introduction of Shylock there begins a full and profound exploration of the effects upon a human being of the Venetians' light worldliness.

Shylock's relation to Venice is shown in the tone and quality of his speech. For the most part the play is set in the polished manner of the Christians, lively, easy, sophisticated, with a marked tendency to playful wit; the effect is to give dominance to their undisturbed and unself-questioning assurance. Shylock speaks as their opposite in nearly every respect. His language is slow, weighted with brooding calculation, reserved and careful, rejecting levity with precision or passion. His is the most resonant voice in the play; and yet it does not disturb or modify the Christians' tone. What it does, however, is to challenge their dominance, by setting gravity against levity and compelling us to perceive more clearly what the latter represents.[1]

In the rendering of Shylock we can distinguish two related emphases. Firstly he shows up and further defines the quality of the Venetians' worldliness. Then he elicits the indifference to human value which underlies it, and which he suffers and returns as an active inhumanity.

In the first exchange in I. iii we are made aware of his subtle seeking for advantage, and also, with a deeper recognition, of the extent of Bassanio's shallowness and selfishness.

Shylock. Antonio shall become bound—well.
Bassanio. May you stead me? Will you pleasure me?
       Shall I know your answer?
Shylock. Three thousand ducats for three months—and Antonio bound.
Bassanio. Your answer to that.
Shylock. Antonio is a good man.

[1] His rejection of the masquers' drums and fife needs a word. It is often set against Lorenzo's invocation to music in Act V and the conclusion drawn that Shylock was closed to heavenly harmony. But what he is rejecting there is rather, as the Lady in *Comus* put it, 'the sound of Riot, and ill manag'd Merriment'. The comparison works both ways, each judges the other.

Bassanio takes this 'good' to reflect upon Antonio's moral reputation; Shylock, surprised at that, patiently explains that his concern is only with Antonio's financial standing. He is frankly using 'good' in the baser sense. At the same time, though, he is spelling out Bassanio's own materialism. For the precise distinction established between mercantile and moral goodness cuts through Bassanio's convenient confusion of them, to show how he is calling upon personal goodness for mere credit. His interest in Antonio is no less mercenary than Shylock confesses his to be.

The exchange should warn us against judging too simply between the Jew and the Christians. It should help us to perceive not only how they judge each other in their apparent unlikeness, (the claim to moral goodness set against the plain materialism), but also how much they are alike beneath the surface differences. What Shylock openly avows, his concern with the wealth of the world, is something he has in common with the Christians.

This relation is developed more fully, though still obliquely, in Shylock's argument for 'thrift' (58-94)—a word that has the place in his speeches that 'fortune' has in the Christians'. The issue is not, as Antonio thinks, whether usury can be justified, but about the ways in which men 'thrive' in the world. Shylock speaks here not so much as an old-style usurer as a new-style capitalist. He anticipates the orthodox Christian view that it is 'against nature' to make barren metal breed, and gives his answer to it by advancing a different and non-Christian idea of nature. The Christian position identifies the laws of nature with the laws of God, so that whatever does not happen naturally cannot be good. Shylock's answer, put very simply, is that it pays to exploit nature. He gives it a biblical sanction in his account of how Jacob prospered 'and was blest', when instead of submitting to nature he found a way to direct it to his own profit. This is to decide what is natural and good by man's 'will' and his 'skill' to make it so, in a manner exactly paralleling the earlier distinction of mercantile from moral goodness.

Antonio attempts to sanctify his own kind of mercantile ventures by claiming that they are 'swayed and fashioned by the hand of heaven'. But this is to confuse Fortune with Providence—as Bassanio had confused credit and virtue. The proper view, recognised in scene i and again in the casket scenes (cf. II. i. 31-38), is that ventures after worldly fortune are subject to Fortune. Bassanio has even used Shylock's word in a significant conjunction with his own—

> I have a mind presages me such thrift,
> That I should questionless be fortunate. (I. i. 175-6)

What emerges then is the likeness of the Christians' practice to that which Antonio condemns in Shylock. In declaring his own position Shylock is revealing theirs.

This must disarm Antonio's prejudiced 'The devil can cite scripture for his purpose'; the remark may even cause us to reflect that his friends are more apt than Shylock at putting a goodly outside on their villainies. By comparison the latter's villainy is almost naïve and innocent, it is so transparent. Not that he is any the better for this. The point of the transparency is to enable us to see the Christians reflected in him as in a glass, but a glass which gives back not the goodly outside but the inward villainy. (For the former we are to have Portia's Belmont.)

Along with this inner resemblance of Christians and Jew we have to consider their radical antipathy, which is of course the most striking aspect of their relationship. The main problem is to give an account of the Christians' hatred of Shylock, for his hatred follows quite naturally from theirs. Here the emphasis is on the inhumanity, which is the more profound and disturbing aspect of their worldliness.

There can be no question that they treat Shylock like a dog, systematically refusing to accept him as a human being equal with themselves. Even Antonio, the best example in the play of Christian friendship, insists that he is and shall remain an enemy, and that there can be no bond between them save a financial one. The main part of Act II (excluding scenes i, vii and ix) is devoted to acting out this attitude to Shylock. Since they do not recognise his humanity the Venetians have neither inhibitions nor a sense of guilt in depriving him of his daughter and his ducats, and then mocking his grief.[1] Their parody of his passion (in II. viii) and their baiting him to his face (in III. i. 25-38) shows the depths of their indifference.

What their actions demonstrate of course is their own inhumanity. Only that word, though strictly appropriate, is rather strong for what we actually see. The Christians remain in their lighthearted element, while it is Shylock whom we see acting truly inhumanly. A clear

[1] The Christian equation of 'gentile' with 'gentle' in these scenes will hardly do, though Kermode accepts it at face-value. The effect of the pun is surely to emphasise the absence of the virtues of 'gentilesse' and civility from the Christians' conduct in this episode.

distinction and distance is thus maintained between their civilised exterior and their real barbarism: we are shown the latter only as it is reflected and returned upon them by Shylock. (This points towards the kind of play this is and the way it works, and is something to be taken up in a general way in the Conclusion.)

That Shylock behaves inhumanly, and that this is a direct consequence of the way the Christians abuse him, hardly needs to be stressed. It is perhaps less obvious that even as he is abused and made inhuman he demonstrates his claim to be treated as a human being. The play prompts us to see his inhumanity as an inverted or perverted form of human nature, and not at all as something apart and devilish.

It is as a man, having like other men 'hands, organs, dimensions, senses, affections, passions' that he feels injured by Jessica's desertion—'my own flesh and blood to rebel!' But inseparable from this passionate cry of outraged humanity is his equal and undiscriminating concern for his lost precious stones. He does deserve Solanio's parody, 'Justice! find the girl! She hath the stones upon her, and the ducats!' His lamentations (III. i. 73-122) are at once elegiac and grotesque. There is the pulse of a profound response, as if she were literally dead to him—'I would that my daughter were dead at my feet, and the jewels in her ear'—but then the wishing her dead that he might recover his wealth makes a shocking mockery of the elegy. The deep movement of feeling becomes attached grotesquely to an unworthy object.

One might say, bearing in mind their common worldliness, that whereas the Christians reduce religious or serious matters to levity, for Shylock, whatever he loves, his daughter or his ducats, he makes a religion of. Thus he can say absurdly and yet convincingly, 'the curse never fell upon our nation till now, I never felt it till now'; for his house is his Israel, and its violation is like a destruction of the temple signifying exile. Shylock does this constantly, expresses some profoundly valuable emotion in a perverted form. He brings us closer than ever the Christians can to an understanding of what it is to be human, even as he puts himself more and more outside humanity. It is as if he discovers and reveals his human nature under the cruel oppression which, as it were, crushes it out of him as it gradually breaks him.

His 'merry bond' with Antonio is the major instance both of the perversion of his humanity, and of his representing in his perversion the inner condition of the Christians. In his lust to be revenged upon

Antonio it is as if he were determined that what the Venetians had deprived him of, his flesh and blood humanity, shall be repaid in Antonio's flesh and blood. Moreover there is a special propriety in his 'I shall have the heart of him if he forfeit', for the heart is the symbol of that life-giving love which Antonio denies him. It comes to seem then that Shylock is desperately and insanely seeking to act out upon Antonio a precise image of the hurt he has himself suffered.

This is the force of the punning upon 'kind' in I. iii. 127-78. There is a fearful obscurity about Shylock's 'This is kind I offer'. The word strongly suggests 'according to nature', and also 'repayment in kind'. With characteristic complacency Antonio and Bassanio read in a moral meaning flattering to their idea of themselves. They assume, as Shylock means them to, that he is renouncing usury and practising instead the liberal generosity they pretend to. But that is just the sense Shylock has refused in his precise way. By using 'kind' which stops awkwardly short of 'kindness' he emphasises that what he is offering is what is according to nature. And in this context, after his own definition of nature, and after Antonio's endorsement of it by refusing to enter into any but a mercantile bond with him, 'kind' can mean only the reverse of 'kindness' or what is proper to human nature. Properly and logically it means his pound of flesh, the heart reduced to meat merely, since it has ceased to be the organ of love. Shylock would do to Antonio precisely what has been done unto him, repaying him in his own 'kind' which has been ungentle and villainous. 'The villainy you teach me I will execute, and it shall go hard but I will better the instruction' (III. i. 66-67).

So far we have established that Shylock is openly what the Christians are beneath their urbane surface. He embodies and elicits the worldliness and the related indifference to the human person which are concealed by their pretence of 'goodness' and 'kindness'. In behaving inhumanly he is acting out the corruption of human nature implicit in their inhuman treatment of him. There remains some unrealised meaning in the situation. There is an apparent inconsistency in Antonio's being at once the ideal Christian friend to Bassanio and the enemy to Shylock. And we have yet to specify the motive and the necessity of the Christians' antipathy to Shylock—we have seen the fact, but not its logic.

Antonio's 'inconsistency' is a matter of 'character'—and within the terms of a character reading it must be inexplicable and unacceptable. For no matter how evil Shylock may be the Christian response should be love and not hatred. However, the difficulty disappears if we stop asking that Antonio should behave with the consistency we expect of people in real life, and allow him to be the dramatic expression of one aspect of the Christian group. We see him then as indeed embodying the principle of charity, which the Christians profess, and in some measure practise among themselves. Certainly Antonio's love for Bassanio is altogether ideal. But we see then that his declaration of enmity to Shylock marks the point at which the principle of charity ceases to be practised. His 'inconsistency' is a dramatic manifestation of the difference between principle and practice among the Christians, and a fuller and clearer statement of what was implicit in his early 'sadness'.

To find a satisfying cause for their rooted antipathy to Shylock we need to put together the several aspects of the play observed so far, and in particular the two central facts: that the Christians pretend to a moral status which is above themselves, and that Shylock avows the moral sense by which they actually live. We can see that in condemning Shylock they are condemning their own sins. It would seem then that they are making him literally their scapegoat, 'all the iniquities of the children of Israel, and all their transgressions in all their sins' having been symbolically laid upon his head. Or, as H. C. Goddard puts it, 'They project on him what they have dismissed from their own consciousness as too disturbing.'

3. 'All that glisters is not gold' (II. i, vii, ix; III. ii)

These are the scenes in which Morocco, Arragon and Bassanio venture for Portia. They are set in the mode of romantic comedy, more purely so than anything else in the play until Act V, and this indicates the quality of meaning we must look for. In Shakespearian comedy the outcome of the events is usually of less interest than their inner significance. The conduct and attitudes of the characters are not judged, as they are in tragedy, in their consequences. Instead the consequences are more or less suspended, while folly or evil is exposed simply for the judgement of clearsighted understanding. The casket scenes (and Act V, but not the play as a whole) are comic in this sense. Their function is to provide a sort of illuminated model of the world of Venice and Belmont. They are set apart from the main action of Shylock and the bond by their blend of courtly poetry and romance; and at the same time they become a sharply defining reflection of that action. If Shylock shows what Venice is like within, Portia's Belmont is its resplendently gilded exterior.

It would be misleading to regard these casket scenes as a distinct sub-plot. We need to think of the play as a whole, in which all the parts are expressing and working out a central preoccupation or vision. Thus the casket scenes draw together and explicate much of what we have already seen of the Christians' worldliness, and provide an advance commentary upon the trial and their triumph in it. In particular Portia's 'skill' in guiding Bassanio's choice of casket is a demonstration of what Shylock praised in Jacob, and a foretaste of the way in which she will have the bond disallowed. More generally, her way with her father's will, which looks back to her own and Gratiano's disregard of the conventional pieties, (and also to Lancelot's and Jessica's unfilial conduct in Act II), anticipates the manner in which the Christians will conform, in trying Shylock, to the merciful will of their Father in Heaven. All the shifts of plot, scene and mode within the play are like the using of different instruments the better to explore the possibilities of a theme.

These scenes amount to a survey of the world subject to fortune. What emerges as the main implication is that the workings of fortune are far from reflecting an ideal moral order. Virtue goes harshly unrewarded, while mere pretence of virtue, aided by 'skill', is crowned with success. Only such fools as Arragon receive their true deserving, which is to be told he is choosing a fool's bliss. The corollary is that nevertheless all will seem duly ordered; the good fortune won by ornament and skill will appear deserved.

The significance of Morocco's fate is that it demonstrates the indifference of fortune to the moral order—as he himself remarks in advance.

> But, alas the while!
> If Hercules and Lichas play at dice
> Which is the better man, the greater throw
> May turn by fortune from the weaker hand:
> So is Alcides beaten by his rage,[1]
> And so may I, blind fortune leading me,
> Miss that which one unworthier may attain,
> And die with grieving. (II. i. 31-38)

Morocco's worth is shown emblematically. Morally speaking he is less like Portia's 'devil' than Blake's 'Little Black Boy'. 'Tawny' is cognate

[1] See 'Note on Texts and Criticism'.

with 'tanned', and suggests the action of the sun on the skin. His opening words develop from this a condensed version of the argument of Blake's poem, claiming to be 'favoured' by the Sun of Heaven and to be in his service, and at the same time to be distinguished in natural energy and virtue. The divine associations would be reinforced by his being dressed 'all in white', which, to an audience accustomed to the use of costume to declare character, would signify moral goodness. The rest of his speech emphasises his nobility as a man: in II. i he is a hero of blood and courage (such as might rescue Portia were she literally 'a virgin tribute paid to the sea monster'); in II. viii he is the Renaissance 'gentleman' and lover, which is the part Bassanio dresses himself for. All in all, then, Morocco is fairly loaded with the emblems and insignia of spiritual and earthly merit, though it is as the gentle lover that he ventures.

In doing so he brings to the proof of fortune the values which Belmont claims particularly to honour. His reflections upon the silver and gold caskets subtly balance courtesy and pride; he does not forget that his object is Portia, as both Arragon and Bassanio do; and he exalts her and the quality of his love by translating the material terms of gold and silver into the most 'gentle' human and spiritual values. Where Bassanio sees her as a golden fleece (in III. ii he even tarnishes that image) Morocco idealises her as 'an angel in a golden bed'. But his idealistic reasoning betrays him. The inscription 'All that glisters is not gold' is hardly a fair judgement upon his own worth—though it may have some relevance to Portia. But its main effect is to place the naïveté of his idealism, with its stern reminder of the nature of the world into which he has rashly ventured. He should have known the irrelevance of thinking by orders and hierarchies of value, and the folly of expecting the outward appearance to correspond to the real value.

Morocco's fortune is clear evidence against the view that the play celebrates an ideal order of things. If any sort of ideal justice were in operation he should be the most deserving of its rewards. What his fortune actually suggests is the likely fate of such as Shylock—the construction of Act II makes this connection, as also does the way in which the references to being prejudiced against 'complexion' (I. ii. 125; II. i. 1) provide a sort of frame for I. iii.—Shylock too being so simple as to expect justice, having chosen fortune and 'skill'.

After the ungentle dismissal of Morocco the cautionary 'All that glisters is not gold' becomes the main burden of the casket scenes.

Arragon repeats it (II. ix. 26-30); and Bassanio's moralising upon
'ornament' (III. ii. 73-107) is virtually a formal rhetorical exercise upon
the theme. By that stage, however, the warning has come to have the
force of a judgement, or of a set of judgements, applicable to Bassanio
himself, to the behaviour of the Christians generally, and particularly to
Portia's conduct of the trial.

Bassanio appears in the most gorgeous fashion of a courtly suitor
(see II. ix. 85-101)—putting on a goodly outside as he has advised
Gratiano to do, and as Portia will do for the trial. This, as he confesses at
III. ii. 253-64, is what Arragon has called 'an undeserved dignity. . . .
To cozen fortune'. His appearance is belied in almost all that he says, so
that he shows up very badly in comparison with Morocco's gentle
courtliness. His meditation on the caskets loses sight of Portia in a fit of
Gratiano-like moralising, in which self-righteousness and cynical dis-
illusionment are sourly blended. His remarks on beauty are especially
inapposite, being a translation into a baser idiom of his first account of
Portia (at I. i. 161-76). The sunny locks which hung on her temple like
a golden fleece are unavoidably recalled and devalued in 'these crispéd
snaky golden locks . . . often known/To be the dowry of a second head,/
The skull that bred them in the sepulchre'; the last image also connects
them with the 'carrion Death' discovered in the golden casket. This
touches Portia much less than it exposes the ignobility of his feeling for
her. The crowning grotesquerie is his effusion upon 'fair Portia's
counterfeit' (114-29)—the sunny locks now become an entrapping
spider's web—where he is clearly fascinated by sterile ornament, and is
excited to ardours which look very strange beside the stilted and halting
couplets in which he addresses the lady herself (139-48).[1]

If our hopes have been set on the success of this callow matinée idol,
we must be shaken in their fulfilment. For his moralisings upon ornament are most clearly relevant to himself, his state nothing, but gilded
with borrowed wealth. More than that, they amount to a revelation of
the world he represents, and a judgement upon it. His winning Portia,
while Morocco suffers the death of noble aspiration, proves only that
fortune loves to be cozened, and keeps a topsy-turvy world.[2]

[1] Cp. the similarly stilted and unfortunate style of his speech to Antonio
in I. i. 122-34.

[2] It has been argued that Bassanio is justly rewarded because he has shown
the proper generosity of love in giving and hazarding all he had. This is to

More important perhaps than Bassanio's undeservingness is the fact that his success is in any case to be attributed to Portia's 'skill'. His meditation begins as if it were drawing a conclusion from the song; the main part of it is not a reasoning about the possibilities, but a rationalisation of that conclusion; the actual choice, when it comes to the point, is perfunctory in the extreme; add to these things the fact that his choosing the lead casket is so little in keeping with his subjection to the eye and ornament, and it becomes quite unbelievable that he should have chosen it unprompted. In any case that the song does give him the hint is plain enough. 'In that age of anagrams and acrostics' the rhymes on '-ed', five of them, together with the invitation in 'Reply, reply' to find another rhyming word, would all suggest the lead casket. To leave no doubt of it the sound of the tolling bell and the references to Fancy dying both evoke the lead in which the dead were folded.[1]

The only reason for supposing Portia not responsible for this very broad hint would be a conviction of her dutifulness.[2] But in I. ii and 1-24 of this scene she has shown on the contrary how her warm-tempered affections are chafing at the restrictions put upon them. All we have seen of her would lead us to expect her to give such a hint, and to give it in this way, keeping to the letter of her father's will. In the manner of Jacob's 'thriving', she observes the terms of the lottery while exerting as much influence on the result as she may.

That Portia should use her skill to have Bassanio win her perhaps has something of a placing effect—her sense of duty is very light indeed if he could outweigh it. Moreover the moral of the song must reflect upon

forget that it is Antonio's 'all' that is in hazard; and to confuse gambling and spiritual generosity. (W. H. Auden has remarked that the only two characters in the play who 'give and hazard all they have' are Shylock and Antonio.)

[1] For most of these points I am indebted to the Cambridge New Shakespeare note, where further evidence may be found. M. C. Bradbrook, in *Themes and Conventions in Elizabethan Tragedy* (p. 110), mentions other Elizabethan plays in which characters reveal in a song what they had sworn to conceal.

[2] Mrs. Jameson's defence of Portia is fairly representative, and as suggestive as spirited: 'Portia *clever*! What an epithet to apply to this heavenly compound of talent, feeling, wisdom, beauty and gentleness! . . . It signifies properly, not so much the possession of high powers as dexterity in the adaptation of certain faculties . . . to a certain end or aim—not always the worthiest.' (*Shakespeare's Heroines*, Bell's edition, 1879, p. 42.)

her as well as upon Bassanio, since both are in love with appearance and
ornament. The implicit warning of the likely fate of such love is not
substantiated, though it is repeated in Act V. The suspicion is there, but
only lightly, that once duty has been subordinated to 'will' there may be
no end to infidelity. Fickleness is, after all, the hallmark of the world of
fortune.

Yet Portia herself is not to be written down as fickle or false. She is
not to be defined by the categories offered by Morocco and Bassanio,
being neither angel nor gilded counterfeit. Instead she emerges with
increasing conviction as a warmly and resourcefully human person.
In III. ii she is first the anxious and tempted woman, in love and not yet
won; then she becomes the more resourceful stage-manager (40-72);
the hint taken, she expresses profound relief and dutiful submission; and
when Antonio's danger is announced it is she who is most actively
concerned to set things right. Her dutiful acceptance of Bassanio as lord
and master (149-75) does tend perhaps to a courtesy-book formality;
it is in the manner of the well-schooled maiden, with a quibbling
rhetoric which prevents any depth of feeling. Yet at the end a true
emotion does break through, validating the simple genuineness of 'You
see me . . . such as I am'. This is a tone of firmer and deeper feeling,
unpretentious and undeceiving—we have just seen her acting her very
natural will, and will be deceived only if we persist in thinking her ideal.
Such a tone is very necessary to redeem these scenes from the disillusion-
ing antinomies of idealism and cynicism.

Thus revealed Portia takes the sting out of 'All that glisters is not gold'.
For in her person worldliness, though limited, is transformed into something positive. She thus requires a fuller and more subtle response than
her suitors. She has transgressed her father's law and forced fortune to
serve her will. But in doing so she has revealed a quality of impulse and
feeling which is not simply selfish, and which is more creative and compelling than either law or fortune. This is not the whole story of course.
Though in these casket scenes she may resolve irreconcilable abstrac-
tions into simple humanity, this is only the prelude to the trial and to
Belmont's triumph in Act V. In these later scenes Bassanio's observations
on law and religion (III. ii. 75-82) may touch her more nearly, and she
may appear less pleasing when she has put on 'the seeming truth'.

The main emphasis of the casket scenes is a cautionary one, warning
against judging by appearance or prejudice. Their constant endeavour

seems to be to prevent our settling upon any fixed or stereotyped basis of judgement. The breaking of Morocco is a breaking of the stereotyped ideal; the rewarding of Bassanio tempts us with a false ideal, and by exposing its falsity even more conclusively breaks the stereotype.

This confusing and contradicting of conventional valuations is most strikingly apparent in the arrangement of the caskets. They appear to correspond to an unworldly hierarchy—a rejection of what the world values in favour of what is least likely to distract the mind from heaven. The trouble with this is that it overlooks the character of Portia, and also the nature of love and marriage. Only a saint would choose the right casket for the right reason; and Portia herself would not then be the appropriate accompaniment. The caskets really offer the inverse of what they appear to offer—appearance and reality cannot be made to correspond. Moreover, whereas the unworldly arrangement inverts the normal worldly expectation, it nevertheless best serves Portia's worldly will by defeating the most noble suitor, and allowing her scope to guide the suitor of her own choice. But this is what one must expect in fortune's realm, where any ideal order is likely to be parodied or exploited for worldly ends, as we were shown in I. i.

In this as in all, Belmont reflects the workings of the Venetians' world in the clear light of its comedy. We are being invited to see through prejudice and illusion and to arrive at a clear-sighted understanding of their worldliness, even as it is recommended to us under its most dazzling appearance.

4. *The Letter of the Law* (*III. iii–v; IV. i*)

It should be possible by this stage to make out the significant structure or 'argument' of the play. We have been introduced, in the early scenes, to a fairly commonplace worldliness, shallow and heartless, but gilded by love of merriment, wealth and beauty. Next, in Shylock, we have seen the perversion of spirit, the blind and destructive egotism, which is the twisted root of worldly 'will'. But again, over that has been laid its most golden appearance, all the pageantry and 'poetry' of Belmont. Thus so far we have had developed and intensified the contradiction between the gilded appearance and the corrupt spirit of the Christians. Now, in IV. i, this conflict of the appearance and the reality is worked out in the bringing to trial and judgement of all that Shylock represents.

If we bear in mind that what Shylock represents is the inward condition of the Christians we may find it an odd resolution which vindicates their apparent virtue in condemning the reflection of their real viciousness. The issues are not as simple as they seem, and for this reason it would be best to begin by asking, in a quite elementary way, what precisely the trial is about, what is at issue and who is to be judged.

Since the moment in Act III when Antonio was known to be forfeit to Shylock, everything has been shaping towards the trial. Antonio's friends, under Portia, have been rallying to him, while Shylock has been shown hardening his heart. At the simplest level, then, we are prepared for a dramatic conflict between Shylock bent upon his pound of flesh and the Christians bent upon saving Antonio.

This simple situation is quickly complicated. The fact that the contest is conducted within the machinery of the law gives Shylock an initial advantage. It is generally allowed that the law and 'credit' of Venice require that Antonio honour his bond. But the Christians introduce a further complication, to their own advantage, by appealing to a higher principle than the law, and translating the issue from the relatively simple legal one into a contest of Justice and Mercy. This shifts the interest all the way from 'who's going to win?' to 'who's good and who's bad?' On the surface everything persuades us to answer this in the Christians' favour. Their identification of themselves with the good, and of Shylock with the bad, confidently assumed in their taking their stand on Mercy, has been suggested to us all along. Most recently Lancelot and Jessica have reminded us (in III. v) that Jews are necessarily damned and that Portia is a saint. Before that we had Portia modestly striking the attitude of Christ releasing the just from hell (III. iv. 10-22). One way and another the Christians would have us believe that the contest is really between the devil and God's elect. So far as we are persuaded of this we will become as anxious as themselves that a means be found to deprive the devil of his base legal advantage. In short, we will become involved in a melodrama.

However, if we are not altogether of the Christians' persuasion, we may see that the melodrama is transformed, in its turn, by the deeper complications of character and conduct. Shylock has shown too much humanity to be written off as the mere devil. The Christians on the other hand have shown too much love of the world, and too much 'skill' in obtaining their will in it under cover of religion, for us to accept them as simple saints. When things go on in the trial as they have before, we can only conclude that the essential conflict is still what it was, and that Mercy is not being practised, but merely invoked as cover for 'will'.

Yet this is not quite the end of the matter. Justice and Mercy, though not what the trial is about, do provide us with the relevant standards by which to judge the conduct of the characters. That Shylock is wrong to stick to justice and refuse mercy is rigorously proved in his own fate.[1] But the larger question is whether the Christians are in truth Christ-like. Ultimately the trial can be seen as a 'proving' of their charity, a bringing of their pretensions to the test of their actual conduct towards Shylock. When they pass judgement on him they themselves are on trial. We may find they have grown genuinely merciful; or we may find them merely mercenary still. But this at any rate is what the trial is about.

A simple but significant point for Shylock's part in the trial is that since he is a merchant like Antonio he should be dressed like him, only with sober decency rather than elegance. To dress him in unkempt black, as producers seem often to do, is only to show him as the Christians would have us see him. (Their prejudice would be sufficiently marked by the tawny-orange headdress which Jews were required to wear in Christendom, until relatively recently—a custom revived by the Nazis.) In this scene it is necessary for a producer to avoid endorsing the stereotyped image of the villain, which is strongly suggested in any case by Gratiano and the Christians generally, and to emphasise rather the complex relation of the 'villain' to Antonio and to his judges.

The essential thing is that Shylock should become terrible. He is not a figure of fun nor an easy butt for prejudice. But everything that makes for his composure, for the self-possession evident in his cool answer to Gratiano's railing (121-42), shows him to be completely alienated from proper human feeling. We can only be horrified by his ebullient trust that the law will sanction his murdering Antonio. Yet his criminality is of the kind which should haunt the conscience of the self-righteous and the complacent, and shock his society into self-recognition. It is

[1] Another indication of the way the action has been translated into a context of justice and mercy, is that no attention is paid here to the natural or poetic justice of Shylock's fate. His abrupt reversal of fortune is consistent with its amorality, which he has chosen to follow; and reflects ironically on his hopeful identification of himself with Jacob, when his part was rather that of Laban. But the workings of fortune are left aside once the higher principle of mercy is invoked: in that context what he deserves in justice ought to be of no account.

impossible not to resist his inhumanity, but it is intolerable that he should have been made so. He is pre-eminently a man in need of mercy; but as for justice, who in the play is fit to cast the first accusation?

There is a grotesque irony in the Christians bidding him show mercy —Hazlitt called it 'the rankest hypocrisy or the blindest prejudice'. For his mercilessness is quite directly the measure of Antonio's refusing to accept him within the human brotherhood. His desires *are* 'wolvish, bloody, starved and ravenous', and this is because the Christians have made them so, infusing their own spirit into him (128-38). Furthermore, there is their common inhumanity in keeping slaves, a practice in con-travention of their principles, which Shylock quite reasonably appeals to as a precedent for the way he proposes to treat Antonio who is now his bond-man (90-102). How should there be any power in the tongues of the Christians stronger than their own example?

Shylock should of course be moved to mercy by his own experience and his reference to the evil of slavery—his own need should teach him the necessity of being merciful. In his inhuman and obdurate refusal to be so he is making himself guilty of his persecutors' crime, and digging a pit for himself. Yet, again, to condemn him they too must unmerci-fully pursue the letter of the law.

That Portia has put on the power and authority of the law, and not anything else, would be declared by the black robes of her disguise, just as effectively as her real nature and interest would be concealed by them. And it would be enforced by her coming on virtually as the answer to Shylock's demand for the justice of the law, and by her meeting and frustrating his demand with a display of deep legal cunning. Of course we are conscious of her as other than the impartial representative of the law. Over and above that is her plea for mercy; beneath it there is her hidden interest on Antonio's behalf. There was also the bawdy masquing spirit in which she talked of the 'device' (= 'an underhand contrivance; a plot, stratagem, trick') by which she would be thought 'accomplished with that we lack' (III. iv. 60ff.). There is so much more to her to be taken into account than meets the eye. We cannot but approve her skilful prevention of Shylock's malice. But we have reason to suspect her motives. And this must make us critical of her large claim to execute the law mercifully and in the spirit of divine charity. That must be tested upon Shylock's great need for mercy above justice. If she is fully to satisfy the expectation she arouses she must respond to his innermost need to be valued and treated as a man. We come again to the recognition that the deepest interest in the trial is in the quality of the Christians' mercy.

The most notable aspect of Portia's speech on that theme is that she quite fails to offer Shylock any motive for mercy, unless the self-interested one of forgiving others in order to be forgiven oneself. The speech is rhetorically excellent, as a forceful rehearsal of the relevant commonplaces,[1] but lacks the one thing necessary, the spirit of love itself. It invites the judgement implied by the allusion in Shylock's 'There is no power in the tongue of man/To alter me': 'Though I speak with the tongues of men and of angels, and have not charity, I am become as sounding brass or a tinkling cymbal' (I Cor. 13).

One of the many sources for the speech is Ecclesiasticus 35, and this provides a useful gloss.

> For the Lord will not be slack, neither will the Mighty be patient toward them, till he have smitten in sunder the loins of the unmerciful, and repaid vengeance to the heathen; till he have taken away the multitude of the proud, and broken the sceptre of the unrighteous; till he have rendered to every man according to his deeds, and to the works of men according to their devices; till he have judged the cause of his people, and made them to rejoice in his mercy. Mercy is seasonable in the time of affliction, as clouds of rain in the time of drought.

That is wonderfully unironic in its reservation of mercy for the self-righteous elect, while storing up vengeance for their enemies—the attitude that makes God a patriot or a sectary. Christ's concept of Mercy, as expressed in the Sermon on the Mount (Matt. V, 43-48; Luke VI, 20-38) wholly transforms that Old Testament one by stressing that God rains his mercy on the just and the unjust alike, and by enjoining his followers to love their enemies. Portia echoes his language, but precisely misses his spirit in neither offering nor asking for love.

There is reason to suppose that Portia is all along preparing to smite in sunder the loins of the unmerciful. Shylock has been assured repeatedly that in law his case is unassailable. Moreover, it has openly been taken for granted that Antonio's blood will be shed; and Portia carries this so far as to bid him have by some surgeon 'To stop his wounds lest he do bleed to death'. All this is to lull Shylock into a false trust in the law so

[1] cp. 'Good sentences, and well pronounced' (I. iii. 9).

that he may be the more surely tripped by its letter. But there is a deeper trap in Portia's words, this time not of Shylock's digging. For as it turns out, she is there tempting him to incriminate himself by an implicit admission that he, an alien, is seeking the life of a citizen (cf. 344ff.). The trick is in bidding him do it 'on your charge', which distracts his attention just as he had distracted Antonio's in proposing the bond, by punning upon 'kind'. It is predictable that he would declare himself under no obligation to spend money on his enemy—why should not his friends provide the surgeon?—and that is enough to put him at the law's mercy.

Portia takes her time, winding him in with the lulling sing-song of 296-300; checking him with her light 'tarry a little'; sardonically urging him to take his pound of flesh, but no drop of blood; mocking him with the assurance he shall have 'justice more than thou desir'st'; then, when he had yielded his claim on Antonio, laying upon him the full rigour of the law. In all this Portia has been practising the law with cunning precision, and to the end not simply of saving Antonio, but of putting Shylock at the mercy of his enemies. There is nowhere any hint of Mercy—and her climactic 'Down therefore, and beg mercy' in no way accords with 'The quality of mercy is not [con]strained'. Simply to force him to release Antonio it would have been enough to show him his danger; to convert him to Mercy in the full sense an example would be necessary. But what we see in Portia's conduct looks most like mercenary vengefulness.

In the event the Christians seem to effect only a variation upon Shylock's scheme to translate the money owed him into heartsblood, by sparing his life but taking his money. This is a transaction no more involving love than his; but it is perhaps the grosser parody. Shylock was seeking a terribly perverted substitute for love, but one at least related to the reality; whereas the Christians neither offer nor seek anything resembling a real relationship with him. Instead they compound for his worldly wealth in order to be well rid of the man. Shylock has no effective retort. His protest, 'you take my life/When you do take the means whereby I live', is too much in character with his previous equation of his daughter and his ducats. Nevertheless we should realise what he cannot, that his tragedy is in the Christians' appropriating to themselves not simply his worldly wealth but 'love's wealth' also. It is their doing that which deprives his life of meaning and value.

All this is imaged in the quibble upon the drop of blood. That drop of blood which Shylock must not shed perfectly represents the love the Christians deny him, the essential life of the spirit. And it is a reminder beyond that of the blood which Christ in his Mercy shed for all mankind. As such the quibble exposes as blasphemous Portia's striking a Christ-like attitude in III. iv. 10-21, and Antonio's playing his sad part upon the stage of the world in the pose of the Ideal Friend laying down his life for his friend with a 'greater love hath no man' gesture (cf. IV. i. 114 and 272ff.). It becomes then the crowning piece in their perversion of their religion that they should require Shylock to become a Christian upon pain of death, imposing upon him the outward form of redemptive mercy while denying him the reality.

Their effective motives and attitudes in the trial are pretty well placed in Gratiano's *Schadenfreude*, his malicious joy in Shylock's undoing, an attitude fully consonant with Antonio's in I. iii, and exactly the opposite of mercy and charity. It is not pretty, therefore, to have the scene close with the spectacle of the Christians being smugly amiable among themselves, assuring themselves of their gentle community with mutual compliments and courtesies. No wonder Portia's 'mercenary' strikes one so: it alone does justice to one's sense of the terrible reality which is being glossed over.

In the end the trial turns out to have been a drama in which the Christians were engaged in resolving their inner contradiction, by casting out Shylock, the scapegoat fashioned in the likeness of their devotion to the world, and a reproach to their indifference to the life of the spirit and the love which it demands. With him undone and compelled to put on their own goodly outside, they are at liberty to enjoy the delights of Belmont, their idyll.

5. 'Love me, and leave me not' (III. ii. 172-218; IV. i. 397-453, ii; V.)

No one will miss the midsummer's night atmosphere of the last act, with the moon making a second day of the night, the poetry of legendary lovers, and the perfecting of the mood by the music brought forth into the air. This idyll of music, moonlight and love is wholly removed from the trial and from everything to do with Shylock, and seems to offer the apotheosis of the love of Venice and Belmont. However, we will find, if our wits are not dreaming, that we are in the same world as before, beneath the moon in fortune's world of 'will' and fickle chance.

There is some passing talk of heavenly harmony, but the last word is Gratiano's, and it resolves the teasing business of the rings and broken vows only in an earthy pun.

Such a conclusion makes sense if we have resisted the temptation to romanticise and idealise the love of the Christians. If we see Bassanio as Ideal Lover, Antonio as Ideal Friend, and Portia as Mercy, it will seem discordant and bathetic. But if we have seen that the Christian group is not ideal, we will discover that the last act draws what has gone before towards its natural *comic* conclusion, by isolating and exposing the real quality of their love. It provides a critique of the love they actually practise, as distinct from that which they pretend to; a love of the world and their own will, sublunary and fickle, not 'ruled as is the universe by divine love'.

The refining and narrowing of the interest in this way accounts for the very different mode and texture. The play is still concerned pre-eminently with the attitudes and conduct of the Christians, but the absence of Shylock precludes any further exploration in depth. Through the main part of the play the fact that the Christians were presented almost entirely through their outward appearance, their social surface and public declarations, was offset by the presence of Shylock, their third dimension. In what the Christians had made him, fashioning their victim in their own image, we could discover what they were beneath their deceptive exterior. Without his substance and depth, and with only the Christians' 'surface' to work on, the writing is inevitably much lighter. Instead of directly engaging our emotions, as in the trial, it now appeals rather to our understanding. There is no conflict or tension in the action; but there are discords and false relations in the poetry. And the main meaning emerges in the way the off-key quibbling of the lovers over the rings jars against the previous evocation of the stillness and deep tranquillity of spirits attentive to love's music.

Probably the clue to a right reading of the last act is the recognition that the allusion to an ideal harmony of love has a critical function, and is not laid as tribute before the Christians. Its effect is not to praise but to place them, to show how far from the ideal they are. Belmont, their paradise of love, is not the heaven of Lorenzo's 'immortal spirits'. It is rather a *very* lightly rendered version (with all the explicit moral pointing left out) of the Temple of Venus in *The Parlement of Fowles*, or The Bower of Bliss in *The Faerie Queene*. The critical intelligence that has been controlling the play is not abruptly suspended in its end. However, its final judgement, in which Shylock is left aside and only the comic mode is used, is subtle, elusive and surprising.

The main stage-business ('action' would be too grand a word) is in the disposing of the lovers' rings. This is preceded by two passages, one on moonstruck lovers (1-24), the other on music and harmony, which establish contexts of literary and philosophical associations within which the matter of the rings is placed.

The first passage offers to create a setting for romantic love:

> The moon shines bright. In such a night as this,
> When the sweet wind did gently kiss the trees,
> And they did make no noise, in such a night . . .

However, all the allusions that follow, seemingly as variations upon that theme of the live and lucent night, undercut its suggestions of tranquil beauty with others of false, or unfortunate or betrayed love. Moreover, it emerges that these gentle lovers are teasingly imputing to each other like infidelities and misfortunes. Cressida's ficklessness, Thisbe's ludicrous fearfulness, Dido's desertion by Aeneas, and Medea's by Jason, are all notorious *exempla* of the fortunes of sublunary lovers. The reference to Medea goes further. If we recall the earlier associations of Bassanio with Jason, it may hint that Portia's fate, in her parallel situation, may be the same as Medea's; for she also has outwitted her father's will to enable a Jason to win the golden fleece, and subsequently exercised her skill to save the life of his friend. The quite direct drawing in of Jessica and Lorenzo themselves to this train of allusions leaves no doubt that they are to be understood as having a cautionary bearing upon the lovers at Belmont. We are being prompted to see that they too fit the old and oft-repeated pattern in which the acting of 'will' against duty is followed by the misfortunes of fickleness or betrayal. The love of the Christians, their pretending to 'gentility' and 'god-like mutual amity', is set delicately and suggestively in a relevant context.

In Lorenzo's speech on the power of music (50-89) we have the opposite context evoked, the harmony of the heavens which are moved by Love, and the analogous harmony of music which may possess even disordered mortal spirits. In gracefully connecting their 'touches of sweet harmony', to which 'soft stillness and the night' are a fitting counterpart, with the music of the spheres suggested by the serene beauty of the stars shining above the night, Lorenzo is establishing the larger term in the analogy. The basic conception is that the stars, as they move in their courses about the Primum Mobile, set up a harmony expressing his perfect ordering of them. This is very richly imagined here, and in a way to realise most compellingly the value of that harmony of being which—for the cherubim whose lord is literally their *illuminatio* —flows from directly knowing the harmonious ordering of things by Love. Fallen man, grossly closed in his 'muddy vesture of decay', neither hears nor is directly influenced by the divine harmony; nor does he (there is this ambiguity in 'doth grossly close it in') attend to the corresponding harmony within his own immortal soul.

Nevertheless music was felt to imitate that harmony of the spheres, and to be capable of exerting an analogous influence. Jessica testifies to this in saying 'I am never merry when I hear sweet music'; and Lorenzo develops the notion in a manner to bring it to bear upon the merry Christians generally. Gratiano and Portia are self-confessedly governed by 'the hot condition of their blood', and Shylock has made us see the wanton masquers as rude animal spirits. Here then are natures which we may hope to see changed 'for the time' by the music of Belmont. It is no accident that Portia's entrance is accompanied by the account of 'That man that hath no music in himself,/Nor is not moved with concord of sweet sounds'. The talk of harmony, even more than the evocations of old lovers, has been preparing a context in which she and her realm may be understood and judged.

Certainly, with Portia's return, we are brought back from thoughts of heavenly harmony to the sublunar world of mortals, as invoked in the opening passage; and then animated, by Stephano's repeating the now much improved joke of her straying about by holy crosses, accompanied by the 'holy hermit' of whom Johnson could not 'perceive the use', and by Lancelot's willing imitation of a courier's post-horn. What emerges almost at once is that music does not still Portia's merry wit, nor make her more attentive to 'sad' feelings (cp. ll. 68–69, 77, and 100–14). There is a harshness and dissonance in her devaluing the lark and the nightingale and making them no better than crow or goose or wren. In the context just established this must make her 'fit for treasons, stratagems, and spoils'—which indeed is pretty much what she has been up to in Venice. Her 'nothing is good, I see, without respect', makes clear where she has brought us; not into the universe where all is ordered by Love and where the degrees of good and evil are steadily distinguished by the cherubim, but into the 'wild and wanton' world of man where all is relative, and good and evil are determined by circumstance and 'will' and 'skill'. These impressions of her being out of accord with the finest feelings and insights touched upon by Lorenzo are confirmed by her stopping the music, as if it were disturbing the peace and not itself the source of the peacefulness, and by her setting up in its place her own tone of brittle merriment (113-32).

Any lingering atmosphere of a world magically transformed by music and moonlight must be fairly curdled by her devaluing the latter as she had the former:

> This night methinks, is but the daylight sick,
> It looks a little paler—'tis a day,
> Such as the day is when the sun is hid.

This gives Bassanio an opening for an elegantly turned compliment, 'We should hold day with the Antipodes,/If you would walk in absence of the sun', which links back with Portia's

> So doth the greater glory dim the less—
> A substitute shines brightly as a king,
> Until a king be by . . .

Her sense there seemed self-congratulatory, even self-glorifying; and she accepts Bassanio's compliment in the same vein, 'Let me give light, but let me not be light'. But this is to pun in the light manner, and her next line slides towards bawdy, 'For a light wife doth make a heavy husband'. This underscores the main effect of the exchange, which is to make us aware of her as substitute rather than ideal. In the trial she made herself substitute for justice and mercy; in Belmont she is a luminary and a centre only because of the absence of the greater glory and true illumination of divine Love and harmony. In the light of that sun her light would appear mere lightness, the sick daylight of tawdry and shallow spirits. This very critical perspective is only lightly suggested and not sustained, but it is sufficiently present to define if not to deflate Belmont.

The main function of the ring byplay, which occupies the rest of the act, seems to be to act out in light comedy the perceptions previously established in the ironies of the poetry. Gratiano has again a significant

part. To the bawdy which Portia's lightness encourages he gives a cruel
edge (cf. 145, 238). In respect of the solemnity of lovers' vows he accurately, if more basely, represents the common feeling, in rating the ring
merely at its material and sentimental value. Nerissa's and Portia's
expostulations and 'exclaiming upon' their husbands, since their tone
observes the decorum of the comic situation, in effect make just as light
of the serious values invoked in the exchange of rings (in III. ii. 172ff.).
When Portia says of Bassanio, 'Even so void is your false heart of truth',
it is not seriously meant, and carries no conviction that his parting with
the ring should 'presage the ruin of [his] love'. In his putting social
before moral 'honour', in self-justification, she finds only an occasion
for the erotic punning (cp. 210 and 233) upon which their comedy is
played out to its happy ending.

The conclusion lets all pass as in a fairy-tale, and crowns their light
play with dreams come true as if fortune had vowed herself to kindness.
In the end their pleasures seem to recommend them above their moral
shortcomings. Possibly Gratiano's urging Nerissa to bed may remind us
of an earlier cynicism—

> O ten times faster Venus' pigeons fly
> To seal love's bonds new-made, than they are wont
> To keep obliged faith unforfeited. (II. vi. 5-7)

Possibly his anxiety about 'keeping safe Nerissa's ring' just hints at the
fates of earthly lovers rehearsed at the beginning of the act. 'Love me,
and leave me not' may come to seem a fitting motto for these light
lovers, its cheap sentiment sharpened by a sense of probable infidelity.
How should love's bonds be honoured when no bond in law or under
heaven but has been made light of?

But it would be a false emphasis to moralise. No serious judgement is
being passed in that form, and no dire fate threatened. We grow aware
of the grave defects in this pleasant comedy only by preserving a sense
of what is absent—those qualities Antonio's 'sadness' portended in the
first scene, and the heavenly harmony so positively if briefly evoked in
this. For example, when Antonio offers to 'be bound again, my soul
upon the forfeit', we need to pinch ourselves with the question, Can he
really be playing at forfeits with his soul? Or again, we have to make an
effort to recall that this apparently inconsequential comedy, which makes
light of faith and inward harmony, has a direct, if hidden, connection

D

with the corrupting and breaking of Shylock. We are likely too to miss the echo, in Antonio's 'Sweet lady, you have given me life and living', of Shylock's 'you take my life/When you do take the means whereby I live'; an echo which might help us to see, beyond the irony of the former's being rewarded with what the latter was mocked for valuing excessively, the deeper connection, in Antonio's being fobbed off with his argosies and denied love's wealth, in the end as in the beginning, just as he had denied it to Shylock.

What we have to do with in all this is not evil but folly, the kind of folly exposed in Erasmus' *In Praise of Folly*, which can lay claim even to the attributes of the God to whom it is blind and indifferent. There is perhaps a measure of direct dramatic judgement of it in the slackening of tension after Portia's entrance, and in the impressions of a coarsening of feeling throughout the business of the rings. It is clearly and consistently placed, moreover, by its association with the moon and the moonstruck lovers, and by its own shallowness and the tawdriness that is inseparable from its superficial wit. But it remains difficult to define the exact quality of our response to it, and to formulate the elusive moral sense that permeates our response. The same difficulty exists for the larger matter of perceiving how this light comedy of folly is a relevant resolution for the play as a whole. The question of what sort of conclusion it is, and, with that, what sort of play it is, has now to be considered.

3. Conclusion

If everyone were out of step with my reading I should have to think again. Happily this is not the case. It is true that it does differ from the majority view in finding, not a simple celebration of the apparently ideal romantic world of Belmont, but rather a subtle exposure of its false pretence. However, there is beneath this broad difference a considerable agreement in matters of detail. Most significantly, nearly all who hold the simpler view recognise that certain important elements in the play can't be reconciled with it. For some it is Shylock's tragic stature, for others the heartlessness and shallowness of the Christians, or Portia's having recourse at crucial moments to an artificial rhetoric. The advantage of the present reading is that it takes account both of the romantic and ideal elements, and of the other very strong element which is opposed to it. It makes possible therefore a reading of the play as a whole; and to do that is to recover its essential drama, which derives so much from the conflict and contradictions of the diverse elements.

However, the comforting thought that my view is perhaps not so much in opposition to the majority one as a more comprehensive synthesis, doesn't much advance the discussion. What best serves that purpose is the direct stimulus of the relatively few critics who also find themselves challenged by the disparity between the ideal appearance and the unideal reality of the Christians. There are three critics whose views are especially helpful here for defining the kind of resolution achieved in the conclusion.[1]

Three Readings of the Irony

Middleton Murry, in his *Shakespeare* (1936), put considerable emphasis on the amoral quality of the last act:

> Antonio and his friends are unconscious. They do not realise any more than did the average decent man of Shakespeare's day, that their morality is essentially no finer than Shylock's, or rather that Shylock's is the logical consequence of their own. Because they are unconscious they are forgiven; where Shylock, being conscious, cannot be. And that is true of life. . . . The decency of an age and an average prevails over the design of an isolated bitterness. (p. 202)

This seems to me very relevantly suggestive, for two reasons. One is the distinction observed between the fully serious judgement of Shylock, and the disengaged, amoral acceptance of the Christians. The second is the perception that this acceptance implies a suspension of absolute moral standards—the standards invoked by many of the critics referred to in the Introduction—and an appeal instead to our more comfortable everyday standards, compromising and compromised, in which such relative notions as 'decency' replace the strict ideal of Charity. I think Murry over-values his 'decent average' and doesn't allow enough for the withering exposure of it by Shylock's tragedy—just as he seems rather too casually disinclined to question the justice of its prevailing over its

[1] I am indebted also, for particular interpretations or for confirmation of my general sense of the play, to B. Ifor Evans, H. C. Goddard, Graham Midgley and Edith Sitwell. For details see 'Note on Texts and Criticisms'.

own 'logical consequence'. But this easy-going forgiveness is in line with his sense that the play is simply 'a fairy story', which would mean that Shylock didn't much matter anyway.

A more equal balance is suggested by a passage in William Empson's *Seven Types of Ambiguity*.[1] He observes that we can make sense of Portia's behaviour only if we accept that she exists on two disengaged planes: she is at one point too 'virtuous' to evade her father's devastating scheme, at another too 'natural' not to; she switches constantly from being the very letter of the law to being quite amorally self-willed. This 'co-existence of contradictions', Empson finds, pervades the play and is the essence of its quality. He calls it 'a form of subdued irony', and defines it as 'a generous scepticism which can believe at once that people are and are not guilty'. My own sense of it would have a different emphasis, perhaps that it allows people to believe themselves not guilty while making it clear that in fact they are. But I particularly value Empson's remarks, which take a position about midway between Middleton Murry's and the one which has emerged in this study, because I suspect that, in resisting the established readings, I may have overstressed the critique of the Christians' morals, and underplayed their 'naturalness'.

My third critic is John B. Shackford, whose account of the play carries the discussion beyond a recognition of the co-existence of contradictions, to a consideration of their dramatic interaction, and so towards the question of how they may be resolved. Shackford first observes that the two different moral senses invite correspondingly different responses. From the viewpoint of the Christians themselves the action is 'a comedy of black-and-white melodrama': 'the black of the stereotype *Jew* is set into melodramatic conflict with the white of the stereotype *Christian*' until 'good triumphs over evil, and all (except the villain) live happily ever after'. But there is the other viewpoint, implied in the very fact of being a follower of Christ, and brought to mind by the many allusions in the dialogue: that of *agape* or Charity, 'the love of the image of God in all men'. From this second viewpoint the treatment of the man Shylock, which had seemed acceptable according to the stereotypes, is found to be tragically wrong. 'Inside the hollow heart of the conventional action the harmonious notes of Christian love echo with ironic discord.' Shackford goes on to ask was Shakespeare deliberately playing to the prejudices of his audience, in order to bring them to the judgement

[1] Chapter 1, 'Annex on Dramatic Irony'.

of a more profound insight? was he practising that form of dramatic irony, in which the satisfaction we may be supposed to feel in the judgement upon Shylock, rebounds in judgement upon our own attitudes, 'for those who have ears and hearts open to perceive the irony?' This does seem to me to get very close to the final effect of the play.[1]

Ironic Comedy

One way of distinguishing the two senses of value in the play would be to relate them to the difference between tragedy and comedy. A rough working distinction in the latter case would be that, in tragedy, the protagonists are exposed to the serious consequences of their folly or error; whereas in comedy the consequences are suspended, and the follies and failings are exposed only to laughter. In these terms it appears that *The Merchant of Venice* is at once not comic and not tragic. It is not comic since the Christian group is exposed to the criticism of the consequences for Shylock of their levity. Yet it is not tragic since it is Shylock who suffers and not themselves. But if the emphasis falls either way it is towards the comic; and this is confirmed in the last act, in which the tragic implications are dismissed, and the Christians left secure in their fool's paradise, unscathed by the evil they have done and at most to be laughed at. We must think of the play then as a comedy; but still we cannot think of it as only a comedy. Combination-terms such as 'tragi-comedy' hardly serve the purpose here. The best term I can find to catch the appropriate emphasis is *ironic comedy*.

I mean the term to indicate the relation of the two moral senses. We are subjected disturbingly to two different and unresolved sorts of justice, two different and unresolved standards of value. This is the main challenge for the producer, or for the reader producing the play in his own imagination: how to preserve the disturbing differences of mode and feeling, and nevertheless to resolve them into a coherent meaning. If they are not preserved the play will be oversimplified; if they are not resolved it will seem an enigma, or simply unsuccessful. It seems to me that the differences are resolved by the operation of a powerful and pervasive irony, an irony which carries into the comedy a seriously critical awareness of what has been felt and understood in the tragic part,

[1] For a note to the point here see Appendix: '*The Jew of Malta* and *The Merchant of Venice*'.

and which, while it does not destroy the comedy, causes us to judge it by values which it fails to comprehend.

For the irony to be effective it is necessary that the tragic and the comic elements be kept distinct and separate—one remarks how naturally they separate out with Shylock's departure. This separateness is, in the first place, a safeguard against melodrama. If the two elements were resolved into a single mode it would almost inevitably support the black *v*. white action described by Shackford. Beyond this, the separateness is positively the condition upon which the two elements are brought into an actively ironic relation. It is precisely by virtue of the clear disparity and opposition, the contradiction of the more profound by the superficial moral sense, that we are roused to seek an appropriate resolution, a unifying vision.

We can get further towards defining the interaction of the two parts by considering the effect of each separately, and then seeing the separate effects in relation to each other. The appeal of the comic part, with its wit, spectacle and diverting plot, is to the eye and ear, to the head rather than the heart. But the tragic part does 'speak to the heart', and engages before anything else our feelings of terror and pity. Our attitudes to Shylock are directly controlled by a quite full emotional response. With Venice and Belmont we must reflect upon the entertaining spectacle in order to discover how we might feel about it; they require our critical attention, but leave our feelings relatively disengaged.

In this difference we have a clue to the dramatic relation of the two parts. Given the Christians alone we could doubtless think our way to a justly judging response. But given Shylock as well we are much more powerfully and directly impelled towards that response. The feelings generated by Shylock must radically influence our sense of the Christians, sharpening and clarifying our attitude to them.

Our feelings instruct us that Shylock is inhuman because inhumanly abused. At the same time we are offered the spectacle of those who abuse him disporting themselves without any trace of guilt. But the play directs us towards a resolution of the disparity by the stronger dramatic force of the tragic part. We discover, I think, that the heart is instructing the head in the right understanding of the comedy, bringing the mind to perceive in the self-centredness and self-satisfaction of the Christians the true cause of Shylock's condition. In consequence what they offer for our diversion ceases to please, for the heart is sensible of its connection with evil. The comedy can only exacerbate this sense, most especially in the last act which follows so closely upon the trial, with the result that it ceases to be simply comic, and becomes transformed by a profound irony.

The resolution effected by this irony is primarily a matter of enabling us to see the bafflingly doublefaced Christians in a single focus, to hold together in the mind's eye their attractive appearance and the vanities and inhumanity which have been exposed beneath it. But the irony then extends beyond the characters, to involve and question the attitudes of the audience, in somewhat the manner suggested by Shackford. So far as we have been attracted to the happily amoral Christians, accepted them at face value, and rejoiced in their good fortune, we may find ourselves exposed, like them, to the criticism of Shylock's fate and of the lesser evocation of a finer harmony.

A restatement of the argument of the previous paragraphs from the standpoint of the last act may show how this could come about. The tone of the ending has much of the ironic reserve of Christ's praise of the bad steward, 'for the children of this world are in their generation wiser than the children of light'. For the several sins of commission and omission which we have witnessed, while they do not disturb Belmont's light happiness, do firmly delimit it, and place it in relation to the grand framework of heaven and hell. We are made aware—though the knowledge is lightly borne—that this happiness depends upon the breaking of Shylock, and the forgetting that he has been broken; and that it depends also upon the breaking of the spirit of divine and natural law, and the forgetting about the spirit under colour of conforming to the letter. If we are invited therefore to recognise and endorse an image of the way we ordinarily live and judge, by the 'decent average', we are shown at the same time the meaning of our complacency. If this is our paradise, it is the paradise of fools.

Yet the most teasing and disturbing quality of the play is that we are left to rejoice there if we will. The unpurged abyss of guilt represented by Shylock, and the unattained heaven of harmonious love, however critical their bearing upon it, may be lightly set aside in Belmont in favour of the moonshine. Yet what is enjoyed in Belmont is attuned to our dreams rather than our necessities, and satisfies no more than our illusions. If we are grateful that the play treats these so kindly, yet the gratification must be slight and shallow. And we can hardly avoid having it soured by the consciousness that it is so. For while the conclusion offers to flatter our fantasies as magazine fiction does, it embodies also, as such fictions rarely do, an ironic comprehension of reality. How many, aware of all that has passed in the play, will rest content with Belmont? and how many will be uncritically content with the standard of average decency in the face of what it could do to Shylock? Our ordinary worldly standards must come to seem less than adequate to the more serious occasions of life touched upon by the play.

Not that the play will purge us of our inadequacies in the matter, or of the follies of the world. Perhaps it would be a more comfortable play if it did in some way or other. Tragedy might purge us of the guilt of being as we are; and comedy reconcile us to ourselves through laughter. But the achievement of this play is in its not fitting cleanly into either mode, and instead confronting us deliberately with an image of our ordinary condition of moral compromise, of complacent spiritual mediocrity. The play neither condemns nor condones that condition: it reflects it accurately, thereby to promote a better knowledge of ourselves. The end makes us aware, even as it invites us to relapse into it, that the cosy amorality in which we would live if we were left to, is not ideal, is not the heaven of perfection we would like to think we aspire to.

We are tempted to look to literature to flatter our illusions of moral grandeur, to show us ourselves in the parts of saint or sinner, hero or martyr. But *The Merchant of Venice* offers to reflect what we are in our ordinary varnished reality. If we find this intolerable it is perhaps because we feel naked without our illusions. The emperor was proud until told he was without clothes.

Upon this ground I would make a final claim for the play—that it has a relevance to life beyond anything we might expect of romance. We have seen that the play does not celebrate a triumph of virtue over vice, but rather instructs the imagination in the deceptions and delusions that may attend upon goodly appearance and romantic prejudice. By thus challenging prejudice, and urging the mind to discriminate more justly between appearance and reality, the play may dispose us to be more properly critical in our own experience.

What is at first baffling and in the end most valuable is the way it complicates and questions a too facile sense of the ordering of good and evil in the world. We have all to a greater or less degree an inbred disposition to equate success with merit, authority with probity, profession with practice; also to suspect the outsider, and to assume that a man formally accused must be guilty. We seem to have a fatal necessity to justify the ways of the world along with the ways of God. All this the experience of the play directly challenges, requiring us to re-examine an apparent equation of success in the world and at law with godliness, and to re-examine also the crude equation of the villain with the devil.

In this the experience of the play might be compared—as lesser with greater—to the experience of many in the '30's, who in spite of a wish to think well of Germany, found themselves forced to reappraise their attitudes to its Nazi government, by the mounting evidence that it employed the language of legality and morality only to mask the most barbarous intentions. On the smaller scale of the morning newspaper such reappraisals are required of us daily. What fraud, folly or abuse of power, what exploitation of the public or expedient betrayal of principle, but is presented by its spokesmen as honest, enlightened, honourable, for the good of the people, and in the interests of world peace? To be particular, and pertinent to the play, consider this contemporary 'sentence' from the propaganda of *apartheid*: you can't treat 'the blacks' as equal because 'their ethics are not ours, and their Christian morals are completely absent'.

The indirect but very real connection of *The Merchant of Venice* with such experiences should be obvious. And, unless we are anxious to dissociate literature from life, we should expect it to be relevantly illuminating for them. We should expect it to be responsively and critically engaged with life as we know it, within the limits only of its particular dramatic mode. That, at any rate, is what it is: responsive to the complexities of experience, critically discriminating among them, and, by extension, critical also of our own tendencies to simplify or to fail to comprehend the experience. The final use of the play, as of all good art, is to make us better acquainted with the world and with ourselves.

Appendix

The Jew of Malta and *The Merchant of Venice*

There are sufficient parallels and echoes of the former in the latter to show that Shakespeare had Marlowe's play somewhere in mind. But once the connection is granted it is the difference that becomes significant. Marlowe's Jew is the stereotype of the villain exaggerated to the height of caricature. Insofar as Shylock is another version of the stage Jew he is an altogether humanised one; with the consequence (noted by Mr. Shackford) that the facile stereotyped response would be evoked only to be challenged. In respect of the Christians Shakespeare has made a perception, which Marlowe reaches only in his last scene, a governing insight of the whole play. At the end of *The Jew of Malta* the machiavel Jew is out-machiavelled by the smoothly god-praising Christian Governor. The effect of this, coming so abruptly and briefly, is that of farce: to reduce an illusory moral order to its proper ruin. Shakespeare's pervasive irony works to a far subtler and more positive effect than that, but is based in the same perception that the seemingly godly may be more villainous than the stage-villain himself. In both matters the differences between the two plays show Shakespeare to have been developing and intensifying Marlowe's relatively simple assault on the conventional stereotypes of villainy and virtue.

Note on Texts and Criticism

I. Texts

Scholars are fairly well agreed that *The Merchant of Venice* was written later than 1594; an entry in the *Stationers' Register* shows it was written before 22 July 1598. The most likely dating is 1596-7.

The text presents few difficulties. There is a good quarto of 1600, 'Printed by J[ames] R[oberts] for Thomas Heyes'. This is the text followed by modern editors, with some corrections suggested by the two other early editions.

Of these the first was a second quarto, printed by Jaggard in 1619, bearing the fraudulent imprint 'Printed by J. Roberts, 1600', and for long taken to be the first quarto. Then there is the text of the 1623 Folio edition of Shakespeare's Works, which was probably a revision of the first quarto, with some reference to the second, and possibly also to lost copy such as the playhouse script.

For quotations and reference I have used the Cambridge 'New Shakespeare' text, edited by John Dover Wilson.

This gives a sound (though not quite perfect) text, with generally helpful notes and glossary. Spelling and punctuation are modernised, as in all editions except the Nonesuch and facsimiles. As the most pleasantly produced and *readable* edition I find it the best for getting at the play itself. (It is marred, however, by the intrusion of some impertinent stage-directions in IV. i and V.) The Cambridge 'Pocket' Shakespeare gives the same text with some alterations, but omits the notes and other editorial apparatus, and fails to indicate the editor's emendations of the text.

For scholarly critical apparatus the best edition is probably now the Arden (revised edition by J. R. Brown, 1955), and this should be consulted, as well as for the notes, on questions of dating, texts and sources, and for a discussion of the play's history on the stage and among the critics. It supersedes the New Variorum, which however contains vastly more information and comment, some of it useful.

Two paperback series which deserve mention for their generally high standard of editing and annotation are 'The Pelican Shakespeare' (published in USA, various editors), and the New American Library's 'Signet Classic Shakespeare'.

The majority of editors since Pope make two emendations which have no authority and which have been shown to weaken the sense.[1] II. i. 35 should read 'So is Alcides beaten by his rage', where 'rage' means 'rash jest, wild folly' (cp. Davies' *Orchestra*, ll. 106-19). For III. v. 72-73 the best reading is probably the Folio's 'And if on earth he do not meane it, it/Is reason'. (Q1 seems to have made the printing error of 'In' for 'Is' in l. 73, which Q2 'corrected' by changing the second 'it' in l. 72 to 'then'.) 'Meane', which is the word modern editors have chosen to emend, refers to 'the golden mean', in a sense contrasting the married state with continence and unchastity (cp. I. ii. 3-8).

2. *Criticism*

I list here only critical writings which have contributed to my thinking about the play. An asterisk indicates those classed in the Introduction as 'romantic or idealising'—it is to the point to recall that both the principal critical editions, the Arden and the Cambridge 'New Shakespeare', are edited and annotated in that spirit.

Barber, C. L., *Shakespeare's Festive Comedy* (New Jersey, 1959)*

Bradbrook, M. C., *Shakespeare and Elizabethan Poetry* (London, 1957)*

Brown, J. R., *Shakespeare and His Comedies* (London, 1957)*

Charlton, H. B., *Shakespearian Comedy* (London, 1938)

Coghill, N., 'The Basis of Shakespearian Comedy', *Essays & Studies*, n.s. III, 1950*

Empson, W., *Seven Types of Ambiguity* (London, 1930)

Evans, B. I., *The Language of Shakespeare's Plays* (London, 1952)

Goddard, H. C., *The Meaning of Shakespeare* (Chicago, 1951)

Kermode, J. F., 'The Mature Comedies' in *The Early Shakespeare* (Stratford upon Avon Studies: 3; London, 1961)*

Knight, G. W., *The Principles of Shakespearian Production* (Pelican, 1949)*

Midgley, G., '*The Merchant of Venice*: A Reconsideration', *Essays in Criticism*, X. ii, 1960, pp. 119-33

Murry, M., *Shakespeare* (London, 1936)

[1] by Hilda M. Hume, *Neophilologus*, Jan. 1957, pp. 46-50.

Pettet, E. C., '*The Merchant of Venice* and the Problem of Usury', *Essays & Studies*, XXXI, 1945★

Shackford, J. B., 'The Bond of Kindness: Shylock's Humanity', *University of Kansas City Review*, Winter 1954, pp. 85-91

Sitwell, E., *A Notebook on William Shakespeare* (London, 1948)

Index